WAIT TILL NEXT YEAR

Doris Kearns Goodwin

Wait Till Next Year

COMPASS PRESS

AN IMPRINT OF WHEELER PUBLISHING, INC.

Published in Large Print by arrangement with Simon & Schuster, Inc. in the United States and Canada.

Wheeler Large Print Book Series.

Set in 16 pt Plantin.

Library of Congress Cataloging-in-Publication Data

Goodwin, Doris Kearns.
    Wait till next year / Doris Kearns Goodwin.
        p. (large print) cm.(Wheeler large print book series)
    ISBN 1-56895-541-3 (hardcover)
    1. Brooklyn Dodgers (Baseball team)—History. 2. Goodwin, Doris Kearns—Childhood and youth. 3. Baseball fans—United States—Biography. 4. Historians—United States—Biography. 5. Large type books.
I. Title. II. Series
[GV875B7   1998]
813'.54—dc21   98-013562

In memory of my parents,
MICHAEL AND HELEN KEARNS,
and to my sisters,
CHARLOTTE AND JEANNE

PREFACE

A few years ago, anxious to enrich his predominantly male cast with a passionate female fan, film-maker Ken Burns interviewed me for his documentary on baseball. I talked about my childhood love for the Brooklyn Dodgers, my desolation when they moved to California, and my becoming a Red Sox fan—a rather ominous progression.

The reaction was startling. Almost everywhere, as I traveled the lecture circuit, I encountered people less anxious to hear my tales of Lyndon Johnson, the Kennedys, or the Roosevelts than they were to share memories of those wondrous days when baseball almost ruled the world. The enthusiastic intensity of their recollections revealed that they were remembering not simply the history of a team or a group of athletes but their own history, and especially their youthful days.

In response, I set out to write a story of my own coming of age as a Brooklyn Dodger fan, a story that would be peopled not by leaders of the nation, but by Jackie Robinson, Roy Campanella, Gil Hodges, Duke Snider, Pee Wee Reese, Sandy Amoros, and the infamous Bobby Thomson.

As I set to work, however, I saw that my early involvement with baseball was an indistinguishable part of my childhood in Rockville Centre, Long Island. Thinking about the Dodgers summoned recollections of my family, my neighborhood, my village, and the evolution of my own sensibilities. I could not talk about my experience as a fan without also telling the story of my life as a young girl reaching adolescence in that deceptively tranquil decade of the nineteen fifties.

From something as simple as the small red scorebook in which I inscribed the narrative of a ball game, I saw the inception of what has become my life's work as a historian. My early friendships, the adventures which took place in my home and on my block, in the butcher shop and the soda fountain, in my church and my school, revealed a microcosm of a time and a way of life shared by many who knew nothing of the Dodgers or even of baseball. These recollections unveiled my own qualities as a young girl, the experiences, the habits of thought and fantasy, the feelings which defined me as a child and which were decisively to shape my life and work as an adult. Thus, my intention to write my baseball story was transformed into something different. I would write my own history of growing up in the fifties—when my neighbors formed an extended family, when television was young, when the street was our common playground, when our lives seemed free from worry, until one remembered the sweeping fears of polio, communist subversion, and the atomic bomb that hung over our childhood days like low-lying clouds.

I soon discovered, however, that my own memory was not equal to my expanding ambition. Some of my most vivid private recollections of people and events seemed ambiguous and fragmentary when subjected to the necessities of public narrative. If I were to be faithful to my tale, it would be necessary to summon to my own history the tools I had acquired in investigating the history of others. I would look for evidence, not simply to confirm my own memory, but to stimulate it and to provide a larger context for my childhood adventures. Thus I sought out the companions of my youth, finding almost everyone who lived on my block, people I hadn't seen for three or four decades. I explored the streets and shops in which I had spent my days, searched the Rockville Centre archives, and read the local newspapers from the fifties. From all this—from my own memory and the extended memory of others, from old pamphlets, documents, yearbooks, and picture albums—I have tried to re-create the life of a young girl growing up in a very special time and circumstance, and set on a path which led inexorably to a place she could not even imagine.

WAIT TILL NEXT YEAR

CHAPTER ONE

When I was six, my father gave me a bright-red scorebook that opened my heart to the game of baseball. After dinner on long summer nights, he would sit beside me in our small enclosed porch to hear my account of that day's Brooklyn Dodger game. Night after night he taught me the odd collection of symbols, numbers, and letters that enable a baseball lover to record every action of the game. Our score sheets had blank boxes in which we could draw our own slanted lines in the form of a diamond as we followed players around the bases. Wherever the baserunner's progress stopped, the line stopped. He instructed me to fill in the unused boxes at the end of each inning with an elaborate checkerboard design which made it absolutely clear who had been the last to bat and who would lead off the next inning. By the time I had mastered the art of scorekeeping, a lasting bond had been forged among my father, baseball, and me.

All through the summer of 1949, my first summer as a fan, I spent my afternoons sitting cross-legged before the squat Philco radio which stood as a permanent fixture on our porch in Rockville Centre, on the South Shore of Long Island, New York. With my scorebook spread before me, I attended Dodger games through the courtly voice of Dodger announcer Red Barber. As he announced the lineup, I carefully printed each player's name in a column on the left side of my sheet. Then, using the standard system my father had taught me, which assigned a number to each position in the field, starting with a "1" for the pitcher and ending with a "9" for the right fielder, I recorded every play. I found it difficult at times to sit still. As the Dodgers came to bat, I would walk around the room, talking to the players as if they were standing in front of me. At critical junctures, I tried to make a bargain, whispering and cajoling while Pee Wee Reese or Duke Snider stepped into the batter's box: "Please, please, get a hit. If you get a hit now, I'll make my bed every day for a week." Sometimes, when the score was close and the opposing team at bat with men on base, I was too agitated to listen. Asking my mother to keep notes, I left the house for a walk around the block, hoping that when I returned the enemy threat would be over, and once again we'd be up at bat. Mostly, however, I stayed at my post, diligently recording each inning so that, when my father returned from his job as bank examiner for the State of New York, I could re-create for him the game he had missed.

When my father came home from the city, he would change from his three-piece suit into long pants and a short-sleeved sport shirt, and come downstairs for the ritual Manhattan cocktail with my mother. Then my parents would summon me for dinner from my play on the street outside our house. All through dinner I had to restrain myself from telling him about the day's game, waiting for the special time to come when we would sit together on the couch, my scorebook on my lap.

"Well, did anything interesting happen today?" he would begin. And even before the daily question was completed I had eagerly launched into my narrative of every play, and almost every pitch, of that afternoon's contest. It never crossed my mind to wonder if, at the close of a day's work, he might find my lengthy account the least bit tedious. For there was mastery as well as pleasure in our nightly ritual. Through my knowledge, I commanded my father's undivided attention, the sign of his love. It would instill in me an early awareness of the power of narrative, which would introduce a lifetime of storytelling, fueled by the naive confidence that others would find me as entertaining as my father did.

Michael Francis Aloysius Kearns, my father, was a short man who appeared much larger on account of his erect bearing, broad chest, and thick neck. He had a ruddy Irish complexion, and his green eyes flashed with humor and vitality. When he smiled his entire face was transformed, radiating enthusiasm and friendliness. He called me "Bubbles," a pet name he had chosen, he told me, because I seemed to enjoy so many things. Anxious to confirm his description, I refused to let my enthusiasm wane, even when I grew tired or grumpy. Thus excitement about things became a habit, a part of my personality, and the expectation that I should enjoy new experiences often engendered the enjoyment itself.

These nightly recountings of the Dodgers' progress provided my first lessons in the narrative art. From the scorebook, with its tight squares of neatly arranged symbols, I could unfold the tale of an entire game and tell a story that seemed to last almost as long as the game itself. At first, I was unable to resist the temptation to skip ahead to an important play in later innings. At times, I grew so excited about a Dodger victory that I blurted out the final score before I had hardly begun. But as I became more experienced in my storytelling, I learned to build a dramatic story with a beginning, middle, and end. Slowly, I learned that if I could recount the game, one batter at a time, inning by inning, without divulging the outcome, I could keep the suspense and my father's interest alive until the very last pitch. Sometimes I pretended that I was the great Red Barber himself, allowing my voice to swell when reporting a home run, quieting to a whisper when the action grew tense, injecting tidbits about the players into my reports. At critical moments, I would jump from the couch to illustrate a ball that turned foul at the last moment or a dropped fly that was scored as an error.

"How many hits did Roy Campanella get?" my dad would ask. Tracing my finger across the horizontal line that represented Campanella's at bats that day, I would count.

"One, two, three. Three hits, a single, a double, and another single." "How many strikeouts for Don Newcombe?" It was easy. I would count the Ks. "One, two...eight. He had eight strikeouts." Then he'd ask me more subtle questions about different plays—whether a strikeout was called or swinging, whether the double play was around the horn, whether the single that won the game was hit to left or right. If I had scored carefully, using the elaborate system he had taught me, I would know the answers. My father pointed to the second inning, where Jackie Robinson had hit a single and then stolen second. There was excitement in his voice. "See, it's all here. While Robinson was dancing off second, he rattled the pitcher so badly that the next two guys walked to load the bases. That's the impact Robinson makes, game after game. Isn't he something?" His smile at such moments inspired me to take my responsibility seriously.

Sometimes, a particular play would trigger in my father a memory of a similar situation in a game when he was young, and he would tell me stories about the Dodgers when he was a boy growing up in Brooklyn. His vivid tales featured strange heroes such as Casey Stengel, Zack Wheat, and Jimmy Johnston. Though it was hard at first to imagine that the Casey Stengel I knew, the manager of the Yankees, with his colorful language and hilarious antics, was the same man as the Dodger outfielder who hit an inside-the-park home run at the first game ever played at

5

Ebbets Field, my father so skillfully stitched together the past and the present that I felt as if I were living in different time zones. If I closed my eyes, I imagined I was at Ebbets Field in the 1920s for that celebrated game when Dodger right fielder Babe Herman hit a double with the bases loaded, and through a series of mishaps on the base paths, three Dodgers ended up at third base at the same time. And I was sitting by my father's side, five years before I was born, when the lights were turned on for the first time at Ebbets Field, the crowd gasping and then cheering as the summer night was transformed into startling day.

When I had finished describing the game, it was time to go to bed, unless I could convince my father to tally each player's batting average, reconfiguring his statistics to reflect the developments of that day's game. If Reese went 3 for 5 and had started the day at .303, my father showed me, by adding and multiplying all the numbers in his head, that his average would rise to .305. If Snider went 0 for 4 and started the day at .301, then his average would dip four points below the .300 mark. If Carl Erskine had let in three runs in seven innings, then my father would multiply three times nine, divide that by the number of innings pitched, and magically tell me whether Erskine's earned-run average had improved or worsened. It was this facility with numbers that had made it possible for my father to pass the civil-service test and become a bank examiner despite leaving school after the eighth grade. And this job had carried him from a Brooklyn tenement to a house with a lawn on Southard Avenue in Rockville Centre.

All through that summer, my father kept from me the knowledge that running box scores appeared in the daily newspapers. He never mentioned that these abbreviated histories had been a staple feature of the sports pages since the nineteenth century and were generally the first thing he and his fellow commuters turned to when they opened the *Daily News* and the *Herald Tribune* in the morning. I believed that, if I did not recount the games he had missed, my father would never have been able to follow our Dodgers the proper way, day by day, play by play, inning by inning. In other words, without me, his love of baseball would be forever unfulfilled.

I had the luck to fall in love with baseball at the start of an era of pure delight for New York fans. In each of the nine seasons from 1949 to 1957—spanning much of my childhood—we would watch one of the three New York teams—the Dodgers, the Giants, or the Yankees—compete in the World Series. In this golden era, the Yankees won five consecutive World Series, the Giants won two pennants and one championship, and my beloved Dodgers won one championship and five pennants, while losing two additional pennants in the last inning of the last game of the season.

In those days before players were free agents,

the starting lineups remained basically intact for years. Fans gave their loyalty to a team, knowing the players they loved would hold the same positions and, year after year, exhibit the same endearing quirks and irritating habits. And what a storied lineup my Dodgers had in the postwar seasons: Roy Campanella started behind the plate, Gil Hodges at first, Jackie Robinson at second, Pee Wee Reese at short, Billy Cox at third, Gene Hermanski in left, Duke Snider in center, and Carl Furillo in right. Half of that lineup—Reese, Robinson, Campanella, and Snider—would eventually be elected to the Hall of Fame; Gil Hodges and Carl Furillo would likely have been enshrined in Cooperstown had they played in any other decade or for any other club. Never would there be a better time to be a Dodger fan.

WHEN I PICTURE MY MOTHER, Helen, she is sitting in her favorite cushioned chair and she is reading. She was slim and tall, several inches taller than my father. Her hair, primly curled with the soft waves of a permanent, was brown touched with gray. She never wore shorts or even slacks. In the grip of the worst heat waves, she wore a girdle, a full slip, and a cotton or linen dress with a bib apron perpetually fixed to her shoulders. Such modesty was the norm in our neighborhood. Indeed, when one of the mothers took to sitting on her front lawn in a halter top and shorts, her behavior startled the block.

My mother had a long face, conspicuously marked by the deep creases and the furrowed brow of a woman twice her age. When she was in her thirties, she was told by her doctor that she had the arteries of a seventy-year-old. Shortly after I was born, she had undergone a hysterectomy after being diagnosed with cancer. Though it turned out that she did not have cancer, the removal of her ovaries and her uterus had precipitated a surgical menopause, which, in those days before hormone replacement, rapidly escalated the aging process. In addition, the rheumatic fever she had suffered as a child had left her heart permanently scarred.

When I was two, she began having angina attacks six to eight times a year, episodes characterized by severe pain on her left side and a temporary loss of consciousness. All we could do, the doctors told us, was break smelling salts under her nose to restore consciousness and leave her on the floor until the pain subsided, which sometimes took several hours. I can still remember the chill I felt from a place so deep within me that my entire body started to tremble when I first saw her stretched out on the floor, a pillow under her head, a blanket over her body. My father assured me that everything would be all right, and said I could sit beside her for a little while and hold her hand. After these "spells," as we euphemistically called them, she would quickly resume her household routine, allowing us to imagine that all was well again.

In our family album there was a photo of my mother in her early twenties, sitting in a chair in her parents' home, her long legs thrown casually over the arm of the chair, her lips parted in the beginning of a smile. Twenty years after that photo was taken, there was in her halting gait and nervous expression scarcely a trace of her former vitality and charm. I used to stare at that picture and try to imagine the high-spirited person she was before I was born, wishing that I could transport myself back in time to meet the young Helen Miller.

Every night, I would fall asleep with the prayer that while I slept the lines on my mother's face would vanish, the leg that now dragged behind her would strengthen, her skin would lose its pallor. During my waking hours, when seated alone, I would daydream, allowing my imagination to reshape those realities I did not wish to accept. In my fantasy, my mother would appear as the young woman in the photo, wearing a summer dress with a ribbon in her hair. She was no longer short of breath, she could run and skip and dance. All my neighbors were crowded together on our lawn to watch my mother jump rope. My friend Eileen Rust and I each held one handle of the striped rope while my mother counted aloud the number of times she could jump without stopping. She jumped and jumped until she reached one hundred, two hundred, and then five hundred, and still she kept going. The strength had returned to her arms and her legs, her cheeks were red. The sun was shining and the wind was blowing, and I was so happy I could hardly breathe.

It was, however, through the older, frailer Helen, not the young woman of my wishful imaginings, that I came to worship the world of books. Whereas my father's interest in reading was confined mainly to newspapers and magazines, my mother read books in every spare moment: books in the middle of the night, when she had trouble breathing; books in the morning, after she cleared the breakfast table; books in the early afternoon, when she finished the housework, shopping, and ironing; books in the late afternoon after preparations for dinner were completed; and, again, books in the evenings.

The corner drugstore had a lending library where current best-sellers could be rented for several cents a day. And in the center of our town stood the cramped public library she adored, an old brick building built before the town had a high school or a bank. With linoleum tiles on the floors, a massive receiving desk, ladders reaching the top shelves, and books spilling out from every corner, our library held a collection begun more than a decade before the village itself was incorporated in 1893. The books my mother read and reread—*Jane Eyre*, *Wuthering Heights*, *Anna Karenina*, *Tales of the South Pacific*, *David Copperfield*—provided a broader, more adventurous world, an escape from the confines of her chronic illness. Her interior life was enriched even as her physical life contracted. If she couldn't change the reality of her situation, she could change her perception of it; she could enter into the lives of the characters in her books, sharing their journeys while she remained seated in her chair.

Every night, after I brushed my teeth and settled into bed, my mother came to read to me. I loved listening to her voice, so much softer and less piercing than mine. She read slowly and deliberately, lingering over the passages she liked, helping me to feel the rhythm of the language, the pleasure in well-chosen words. She modulated her voice to reflect the different characters and the pace of the narration. Rudyard Kipling was one of my favorite writers. I took to heart the motto of the ever-curious mongoose family in "Rikki-tikki-tavi"—"Run and Find Out." Everything was investigated firsthand; hearsay meant nothing. If there was an inkwell on the writer's desk, then Rikki-tikki's whiskers would be stained with the blackest India ink; if there was a rustle in the garden, Rikki-tikki's eyes would glow with anticipation.

From the *Just So Stories,* I learned how the camel got his hump, how the rhinoceros got his skin, and, best of all, how the elephant got his trunk. At the start of the story, the elephant had only a bulging nose, no bigger than a boot, incapable of picking up anything. Just as I identified with the intrepid mongoose, so I empathized with the elephant's child, full of a "satiable curiosity" which irritated everyone around him. He asked the ostrich why her tail feathers grew, and the ostrich spanked him. He asked the hippo why her eyes were red, and the hippo spanked him. He asked everyone what the crocodile ate for dinner and, finding no answer, ventured to the riverbank, where he ended up in the crocodile's mouth. His friend the snake hitched himself around the elephant's hind legs and told him to pull as hard as he could to save himself, and as the little elephant pulled, his nose began to stretch and kept on stretching. By the time the crocodile finally let go, the elephant had a full-grown trunk. Thus curiosity was abundantly rewarded.

The young Thomas Edison, like the elephant, the mongoose, and me, was relentlessly curious. I had come to know him through the Blue Biography series, which my mother read to me in its entirety. Written for children, this classic series focused on the childhoods of famous Americans, including Abraham Lincoln, Susan B. Anthony, Benjamin Franklin, George Washington, Betsy Ross. But Edison, so full of energy and elaborate plans, fascinated me the most. At one point, he decided to read all the books in the town library, one shelf at a time, something I could easily imagine wanting to do myself once I had learned to read. And he, too, was always questioning his parents and teachers. He wanted to know why he saw lightning before he heard thunder, why water couldn't run uphill, why some parts of the ice pond were lighter than others.

But I suppose my fascination with Edison was fueled by the knowledge that when my mother was sixteen she had worked as the private secretary to the president of the New York Edison Company. It was her first job after graduating from secretarial school. I pictured her walking swiftly through the streets of Manhattan in tailored clothes with high heels, to take her place behind a big desk in a tall building. In my imagination, she worked directly for Thomas Alva Edison himself, as his gal Friday. I envisioned her at Edison's side in his laboratory when he invented the phonograph and the electric light. She would try to set me straight on chronology, informing me that she hadn't even been born when these inventions were made, but I refused to let her corrections disrupt the dramatic narrative I was writing in my head. Every year, on the eleventh of February, Edison's birthday, I made up Alva buttons for the family. I cut out circles of poster board and pasted a picture of Edison on the front with the name "Alva" in big red letters along the top. The name "Alva" intrigued me, and I liked the thought that my mother knew him so well she would call him by that exotic name.

The only joy that surpassed listening to a book read aloud was listening to real stories of my mother's youth. "Tell me a story," I would beg, "a story about you when you were my age." She told me stories about her father, who was a ferryboat captain operating between Weehawken and Hoboken; stories about her mother, whose parents had emigrated from England, and her uncle Willy, also a ferryboat cap-

14

tain, who had fought in the Great War and traveled halfway around the world. There must have been some money on my maternal grandmother's side. My mother always referred to the house she grew up in as "the Mansion," and she talked about an uncle who was a successful artist, who did all the frescoes for the famous Hippodrome theater on 43rd Street in New York City.

She told me about her twin brothers, who died at the age of two during a cholera epidemic that swept through New York in 1906, shortly before she was born. The two little boys were laid out on a cherrywood table in the parlor of her parents' home. Ever after, when I passed the elegant table, which now stood in the corner of our dining room, I pictured two round-faced cherubs waiting in heaven for the rest of their family to join them. Thus the table became, not a reminder of death, but a platform to paradise.

I pressed her to tell me every detail about her first meeting with my father. "The first time I saw your father, he was standing at the door to our house. He had come to pick up my brother, Frank, who was his best friend." I wanted to add to her story, to have her tell me that the moment she saw him she knew that this was the man with whom she wanted to spend the rest of her life. Unfortunately for the story I was spinning in my head, she was only fourteen when they first met. "But what about Dad? He was nineteen, right? Didn't he know the first time he saw you?" "Perhaps." She smiled. "But it was a few years before he stopped thinking of me as Frankie's kid sister and realized I was a young woman. We were friends first and only later fell in love. That's the best way, I think." I nodded agreement, though I could never completely give up the notion that romantic love struck like a bolt of lightning.

As we talked about the past, she seemed to forget her pains. Her eyes brightened, and when she smiled, the creases at her mouth turned upward, giving her face a look of relaxation and warmth it did not usually have. I came to believe that, if only I could keep her youthful memories alive, if I could get the happy thoughts of her girlhood to push the sadder thoughts of her womanhood away, I could prevent the aging process from prematurely moving forward. In my imagination, the brain was a finite space with room for only a certain number of thoughts, so it was critical to push the bad thoughts out to leave space for the good ones. And somehow, on the strength of the changed expression on my mother's face, I assumed there was a direct correlation between one's inner thoughts and one's outer well-being. It made me so happy to see contentment on her face that I reached out to stories of the time she was young and vital as if they were lifeboats that would carry my mother through the present into the future. Through her stories, I could imagine her young again, taking the stairs two at a time. Even now, when I interview people for my books, it sometimes seems I am sitting with my mother pleading, "Tell me a story."

As a child, I loved looking through my mother's photo albums. Through a series of faded pictures attached by sticky corners to the pages, I discovered Ephraim and Clara Miller, the maternal grandparents I had never known, and my uncle Frank, who had died a few years before I was born. My mother told me she had considered her mother her "best friend in the world." When she worked at Edison, they spent every Saturday together. They would go shopping, eat lunch, and go to the movies. After my parents married and moved to East 64th Street in Brooklyn, my mother's parents moved into a house on East 63rd Street. When my sister Charlotte was born, my grandmother virtually lived at our house, helping to care for the baby, cook the meals, and keep my mother company. I stared at the pictures of my grandparents, both heavy people with kindly smiles, and imagined what our life would be like if they were living next door. I had never met either one of them, for they had died, suddenly, within three weeks of each other, when they were in their early fifties. My grandfather died first, of a heart attack. Three weeks later, my grandmother went into postoperative shock after what should have been routine gall-bladder surgery. She died the following morning. My mother was only twenty-two at the time.

One day, while my mother and I were looking through the album, she was called to the phone. In her absence, I decided that the pictures needed a little brightening. Taking my crayons, I colored a photograph of my mother and grandmother taken when my mother was in her teens, my grandmother in her forties. Standing side by side, they squinted in the sun, arms resting comfortably on each other's shoulders. With my red crayon, I gave my grandmother rosy cheeks and big lips and then colored her hair yellow so it would match mine. When my mother came back and saw the picture, she was so angry she could hardly speak. "But she looked so pale," I tried to explain, having no idea what I had done to make my mother so upset.

"THERE ARE SOME THINGS we don't ask," my mother said, a harsh tone in her voice when she heard me pestering my father to tell me about his early life. I knew that he'd been born in Brooklyn on September 6, 1901, the day President William McKinley was assassinated by a Polish American anarchist, Leon Czolgosz. He liked to say that, though the newspapers that day carried the full story of the assassination, the headline story was the birth of Mike Kearns. I knew that his parents, Thomas Kearns and Ellen Higgins, had emigrated to the States from County Sligo, Ireland, and that his father worked as a fireman in Brooklyn. And I knew that Thomas and Ellen had died when my father was young, but whenever I asked for more details about his family, his eyes took on a guarded expression, and a look of pain settled around his mouth. It was the only time

I felt uncomfortable around my father, as if some chasm stretched between us.

When I turned to my mother for answers, she filled in the picture of my father's childhood, but only after I had promised not to talk with my father about it. She told me that his entire world had collapsed when he was nine years old, that it was better for him to leave his pain behind him, and that I must respect his wishes. The story as I understood it was as follows: My father was the oldest in a family that once included two brothers, Thomas Jr. and John, and a sister, Marguerite. They lived at 633 Myrtle Avenue, a two-story tenement house shared by four families whose living quarters were separated by thin, temporary walls. Myrtle Avenue was a congested street with an elevated train running above a trolley line. The noise of the el was so constant that people noticed only when it stopped. But relief was always possible, my father told my mother, for nearby stood Fort Greene Park, a stately public space with its double row of blossoming chestnut trees that stood in defiant contrast to their bleak surroundings.

Thomas Jr. died at fifteen months. Then, in the summer of 1910, when my father was eight, his five-year-old brother, John, was hit by a trolley car. The deep wound in John's left leg produced a deadly form of tetanus that led to spasms and convulsions and finally left him unable to breathe. He died, in the middle of July, when their mother was five months pregnant. Her grief produced complications in the pregnancy, which led to her own death in November at the age of thirty-seven. Then, less than two months later, shortly after the Christmas holidays, my father's father died. He was forty years old.

In my imagination I linked these events into one continuous story. First my father's little brothers died, then his mother died in childbirth, and then his father died of a broken heart. In the absence of facts, I expanded upon the saga. I pictured my grandfather trying to be both father and mother to his two remaining children, fighting fires during the day, then racing home at night to cook dinner, do the laundry, clean the house, read to the children, and tuck them into bed. At some point, I assumed, he had simply collapsed from the strain and died. It was not until much later, after my own mother died, that I discovered how much more complicated the real story was.

Left as orphans, my father and his four-year-old sister, Marguerite, were split up and sent to live with relatives in different parts of Brooklyn. I am told that my father went to see her almost every night, and promised that he would someday find a place and secure the means for the two of them to live together. He kept his promise. Before he was eighteen years old, he had a job as a runner on Wall Street, which enabled him to reunite the remnants of his family for a short moment in a small apartment on Monroe Street. For three years, he and his sister lived together while she finished school and got a clerical job. Then the almost unbearable chain of events that had begun with his brother's accident, this grim net which had captured his childhood, fell upon his sister. When Marguerite was sixteen, a freak accident with anesthesia administered during a simple dental procedure led to complications and, ten days later, she was dead. In the space of little more than a decade, my father had lost his two brothers, his mother, his father, and, finally, his sister.

When my father did speak of his family, he spoke only of his younger sister, and always with great affection. Rather than dwelling on the tragic absurdity of her death, he focused on the reddish tint of her hair, her high coloring, her warmth, and her ease with people. Over the years, I felt a strong connection to Marguerite, in part because of our similar complexion, in part because of our common position as the youngest in our families, but mostly because my father loved her so much. When I was about to be confirmed in the Catholic Church at the age of eleven, my father asked me to take the name of Marguerite as my confirmation name. It was an easy request, for this was the name I had come to want for myself.

For reasons that I will never fully comprehend, my father somehow emerged from this haunted childhood without a trace of self-pity or rancor; on the contrary, he seemed to possess an absolute self-confidence and a remarkable ability to transmit his ebullience and optimism to others. There is an old Jesuit maxim: "Give me the child for the first seven years and he will be mine for the rest of his life." Perhaps the love he was given by his parents in his early years gave him the resources he needed to confront the trials he later faced. Or perhaps he was simply born with a sanguine temperament, a constellation of positive attitudes that became as much a part of his makeup as the color of his eyes and the shape of his nose. What is clear is that at some point my father determined he would write the story of his life himself, rather than let it be written for him by his tortured past. And this resolve was the greatest gift he bequeathed to his children.

My PARENTS had not planned on having me. With two daughters, Charlotte, fourteen, and Jeanne, nine, they thought their family complete. Charlotte later told me she was so embarrassed to discover our mother's pregnancy at the advanced age of thirty-five that she refused to tell her high-school friends. On the day I was born, a blustery January day in 1943, my father handed out cigars to his fellow examiners and bankers. One of these colleagues was the father of a high-school friend of Charlotte's. When the girl arrived at school the next day and told everyone the news, Charlotte was mortified. Her only hope, she would later tease me, was that I be shut away in the attic until I was grown.

Everything glamorous, comely, elegant, fragrant, remote, feminine, and forbidden was my sister Charlotte for me. She seemed the model of physical perfection, tall and shapely, with high cheekbones, a creamy complexion, large hazel eyes, and long thick hair. She walked with a natural grace and wore a slight smile that seemed to acknowledge her beauty. The star in her high-school plays, she thrived on attention and was always conscious of her appearance. During one play she refused to dye her hair gray, fearing it would make her look old at the cast party later that night. I remember her surrounded by adoring boys—one had a Chrysler Highlander with a plush red interior, another a violet Chevy he called the "Purple Passion."

Once, when she was still in high school, Charlotte told us that the new boyfriend she was bringing home had an ugly scar on his right cheek, about which he was acutely self-conscious. She warned us against looking directly at his face when she introduced him. I tried to obey her command, but my eyes were drawn irresistibly to his forbidden right cheek. Seeing no scar, thinking I must have confused right and left, I maneuvered to his other side, which was equally unmarred. Later that night, I asked my sister why she had told us the story of the scar. "He's so arrogant about his good looks," she replied laughingly, "that I figured it would throw him off if none of you looked at his face."

I liked to sit on a small cushioned stool in

the back bedroom, which my sisters shared, and watch them get ready for their dates. Jeanne was shorter than Charlotte by more than half a foot, but had the same dark hair, thick brows, and large eyes. They shared a dressing table with a fluffy white organdy skirt, arrayed with brushes, combs, tweezers, emery boards, and colognes. I watched in admiring bewilderment as they brushed their hair, fifty strokes at each sitting, and put cold cream on their faces. And I can still see, reflected in the vanity mirror, the expression of discomfort on their faces as they held one eyebrow taut to tweeze imperfect hairs from their perfectly shaped brows. I was something of a tomboy, more comfortable in pants than dresses, with skin that freckled and blistered in the sun. I could not imagine that the day would ever come when I would voluntarily put myself through pain for the sake of beauty.

After Charlotte finished high school, she entered a three-year diploma program at Lenox Hill Hospital in New York to become a registered nurse. She had picked nursing, she liked to say with an ironic turn of her lip, because, "besides saving lives and all that other noble stuff, I'll get to wear a great uniform—all white, freshly starched each day, with long sleeves, French cuffs, and matching stockings." When I was five, I accompanied my family to Charlotte's capping ceremony, which symbolized the end of her six-month probation period and the beginning of the intensive training to become a nurse. Emerging from the train station, I was overwhelmed by the wondrously mingled noises, the sound of police whistles and the multitude of cars rumbling along the streets, and the crowds of shoppers hurrying past the vast and glistening window displays.

The ceremony was beautiful. About sixty student nurses marched in a solemn line toward the stage, lighted candles in hand. The glow from the candles cast a strange and wonderful light on their faces. "Why are they carrying candles?" I whispered in a loud voice to my mother. She explained that the candles were in honor of Florence Nightingale, the founder of the nursing profession, who carried a burning light as she tended to the wounded soldiers in a makeshift military hospital during the Crimean War, earning herself the name "Lady with the Lamp." When Charlotte's name was called, she walked to the center of the stage, where she received a white bib with "Miss Kearns" embroidered on top in blue letters, and an organdy cap with a ruffled back which looked like a miniature chef's hat. I was so excited I stood up and cheered, shouting her name as if she had just hit a home run.

The next summer, when I was six, Charlotte took me to Rockefeller Center and Radio City Music Hall. Before we left the house that morning, she used the curling iron on my hair until the strands on both sides curled up evenly. Unfortunately, before we reached the train station, one lock on the right side drooped downward—the same rogue piece that appeared that year in my first-grade photo, giving me a page boy on one side and a flip on the other. Our first stop was Saks Fifth Avenue, where Charlotte planned on buying me a new dress. As we walked up Fifth toward 49th, the rhythmic click of my sister's alligator shoes on the sidewalk seemed to draw the attention of everybody nearby, even the poodles on their leashes and the mannequins in the store windows. At Saks, she knew exactly what she wanted for me; I had to try on only two dresses to find a light-blue one we both loved. From that moment, I valued her opinion on style far more than my own. It was she who taught me not to wear pink with red, not to combine plaids and polka dots, not to wear white past Labor Day. If I didn't always follow the rules, at least Charlotte had made me everlastingly aware of them.

Entering Radio City Music Hall for the first time, I was amazed by its majestic foyer, its grand stairway and gold-leaf ceiling. The auditorium, seating more than six thousand patrons, was vaster than any public space I had ever seen. The spectacle was dazzling—the world's largest theater orchestra, plus the Rockettes, the world's finest precision dancers, and a movie, *In the Good Old Summertime*, with Judy Garland and Van Johnson, on the world's largest screen. After the movie, we went to Toffenetti's for ice cream. As we sipped our sodas, I noticed that the eyes of four boys at the next table were fixed on my sister. They were dressed in white uniforms—Annapolis boys, it turned out—and they whispered together, casting sidelong glances at our table. As we were about to leave, a big teddy bear arrived for me with a note saying they hoped I'd grow up to be as beautiful as my mother. I could not help feeling a rush of joy at the thought that these handsome fellows assumed I was Charlotte's child and that I might some-day look like her. I fervently wished at that moment that I had a mother who looked like my older sister instead of a grandmother.

Much later that night, I was abruptly awak-ened by a thunderclap and a flash of lightning outside. The rumble of the storm grew more and more insistent and I could not go to sleep. I called to my mother, and straightaway she appeared in her thin blue robe, to rearrange my bedding and stroke my forehead, her warm, familiar voice gently comforting me. I remembered the four cadets earlier in the day and my guilty wish for a different mother. Tears came into my eyes, and a deep sense of shame that lay like a physical weight on my chest. "Don't be frightened," my mother said. "The storm will pass in a few minutes, and I'll stay with you till it does."

IF CHARLOTTE was a distant ideal, living as she did away from home through most of my childhood, Jeanne was an everyday presence. For as long as I can remember, she was a surrogate mother, looking out for me, taking care of me when our mother was sick. The nearly ten-year gap in our ages eliminated the potential for competition and defined our roles: she was the grown-up; I was the kid sister. Loving, patient, and gentle, she gave to me more than I gave her in return. Whatever hesitations she must have had about taking responsibility for me, she always made me feel as if she had been waiting for a little sister all her life.

In the summer of 1949, Jeanne was sixteen, about to enter her junior year in high school. She was one of the top students in her class: vice-president of the student organization, treasurer of her Hi-Y club, president of the dramatic club, and leader of a service organization that gathered canned goods for needy families in the Deep South and knitted afghans for veterans' hospitals. Though I had no idea why the people in the Deep South needed food, I got so caught up in the canned-goods drive that, each time I went to the corner store for my mother, I would bring home an extra can of soup and hide it under my bed. When my hidden cans added up to a dozen, I proudly presented them to my sister as my contribution to the overall effort, taking immense pleasure in the thought that my hoarded cans would soon appear on the kitchen table of families far away.

I tagged along with Jeanne everywhere—to the movies, the beach, the houses of her friends. There must have been times when I aggravated her, but she was never openly resentful, and only rarely bossy. On rainy Saturdays, she patiently took me with her to the movies, where she and her girlfriends talked with each other and flirted with the boys. We had two movie theaters in Rockville Centre: the Strand, which had once been a vaudeville house, boasting a live orchestra and a Wurlitzer pipe organ, and the newer Fantasy Theatre, an ornate picture palace designed in an Egyptian motif at the time King Tut's tomb was found, with a deep balcony, lush carpeting, and matrons dressed in black. As long as I kept relatively quiet and curbed my natural tendency to plunge into any conversation—especially when the boys turned the talk to baseball—she let me sit by her side. She remembered that, when she had gone to the movies with Charlotte, she was forced to walk several paces behind Charlotte and sit by herself seven rows to the rear of Charlotte's group. No exception was allowed, and Charlotte had warned her that if she told our mother about their arrangements she would be committing a mortal sin in the eyes of the church, called "tattletaling." The routine continued until Jeanne, in preparation for her First Communion, went to First Confession. She told the priest of her temptation to tell her mother about her unhappiness, though she knew it was a mortal sin to tattle. The priest laughed, and told her she needn't worry. Tattletaling was not a mortal sin. When Jeanne emerged from the confessional with a big smile on her face, Charlotte knew the jig was up. From that day forward, she had to let Jeanne walk beside her on the sidewalk and sit next to her at the movies.

Jeanne also let me accompany her when she and her friends went to Jones Beach, which remains the finest beach I have ever seen, finer than the exclusive resorts on the Caribbean, finer than the private beaches in Malibu. Jones Beach was not just sand and water but a world-class public resort, "a kind of people's palace or people's country club," as critic Paul Goldberger once described it, "as careful and determined in its symbolism as a seat of government." Completed in 1929 under the leadership of New York Parks Commissioner Robert Moses, it was unparalleled as a design for public space: six miles of perfectly kept snowy white sand, two giant bathhouses, two large, heated, saltwater pools for fifteen thousand swimmers, dressing rooms, lockers, beach shops, comfort stations, five cafeterias, and a marine dining room. A paradise for children and grown-ups alike, it contained two ice-cream parlors, a roller-skating rink, an outdoor dance floor, an Indian Village, and a mile-long boardwalk with a pitch-and-putt golf course, shuffleboard, Ping-Pong, handball, paddle tennis, and archery.

Approaching the beach from the parkway, we knew we were drawing near as soon as we caught a glimpse of the giant red brick water tower that stood as the symbol of the park and could be seen for many miles on a clear day. I caught my breath in anticipation not unmarked by apprehension every time I saw the tower, which stood nearly two hundred feet high and resembled a Venetian campanile. Though the tower presaged our arrival at the beach, it also had an aura of menace: I had been told that this tower was in fact a prison where little kids were held if they did not obey their elders at the beach. I could never figure out how the kids were lowered into the tower, or what they did once they were inside, but I did not pursue my curiosity, deciding it was better not to know too many details.

Our parking lot was Number Four, connected to the beach and the bathhouses by an underground tunnel that formed an echo chamber if you shouted "helloooo," as we invariably did. Emerging from the tunnel, we were greeted by a fabulous display of petunias and, if we were lucky, five or six cottontail bunnies scurrying amidst the flowers. My favorite sight was the Art Deco poolhouse, a veritable castle of red and tan brick that held the magnificent pools. My sister and her friends preferred the ocean beach. Radios settled carefully on the edge of their blankets, they lay for hours, securing their tans, flirting with boys, and reading love stories in *True Confessions*. Every now and then they would stir from their lethargy to add a layer of their favorite tanning concoction, a mixture of baby oil, iodine, and cocoa butter. When the heat of the sun became unbearable, they would dip themselves in the ocean for a minute or two and then slowly saunter back to the blanket, hoping to lure the orange-and-black-suited lifeguards from their perches in their high double chairs.

As soon as I knew where on the beach my sister's blanket was located, I raced to the tunnel that led to the pool. Inside, the smell of the chlorine produced a feeling of happy intoxication which lingered even as I emerged into the open and was momentarily blinded by the brilliant light reflected from the blue water, gleaming diving boards, and white balcony. Jeanne was the one who had taught me how to swim, and she knew that I could handle the pool on my own. Surrounded by hundreds of fellow swimmers, I would stay in the pool for hours, paddling up and down the lanes, or clinging to the side and watching as people dove off the high diving board. Though Jeanne could dive frontward and backward off the highest board, I never learned to dive, and I watched the graceful plunges of other swimmers with awe.

Jones Beach also became the setting for a new friendship in that summer of 1949. Johnny was eight years old. He had blue eyes and curly hair. Not only was he a Dodger fan, but he knew far more about the Dodgers than I did, perhaps because of his two-year seniority. My small stock of stories and fables was far outdistanced by what seemed to me a truly breathtaking knowledge of the team and its history, derived, like mine, from his father and his family. It was my first introduction to the invisible community of baseball, which now, for the first time, was extended beyond my street in Rockville Centre, to the town of Mineola, where Johnny lived. In years to come, I would find that the lovers of the Dodgers, and, indeed, of baseball, shared common ground, reaching across generations and different social stations dispersed across the country. Even now, wherever I travel on a book tour or to give a lecture, I invariably encounter an old Dodger fan, or the child of a fan, eager to exchange stories laden with that mingled pain and exultation which was the shared lot of every Brooklyn follower.

It was Johnny who first told me the story of the 1941 World Series between the Dodgers and the Yankees, when Dodger catcher Mickey Owen dropped the third strike, a story I was to hear many times from many people, all ritually re-enacting the tragedy which the years had translated into strange delight. The Yanks had won two of the first three games, but in the fourth game, the Dodgers were leading 4–3 in the bottom of the ninth with two outs and no one on base. Tommy Henrich stepped to the plate to face Dodger reliever Hugh Casey. Casey quickly got two strikes on Henrich and then threw a wicked curve, which may have been a spitball, which Henrich swung at and completely missed. The game was over and the Dodgers had won, the Series was tied at two games apiece— or so it seemed, until it became clear that Mickey Owen had been unable to catch the third strike. In fact, the dropped third strike had rolled all the way to the backstop behind home plate, and Henrich had reached first base safely. The Yankees made the most of their opportunity: the next batter walked, and the batter after him doubled. The Yankees won the game and eventually the Series.

Ever the fantasist, in my imagination I would stop the action at the point where Casey was about to throw the third strike. This time Owen caught the pitch, the third out was recorded, and the Dodgers went on to become champions of the world. I wondered how many times Mickey Owen himself had replayed that same moment in his mind and tried to force a different ending. I felt terrible for him. Years later, I learned that he was never really the same afterward and that Hugh Casey eventually became a heavy drinker and killed himself with a shotgun blast in his hotel room.

But for every tale of woe there was a tale of joy, and nothing gave me greater happiness than talking with Johnny about our shared hero, Jackie Robinson. Johnny had been to several games in 1947, the historic season when Robinson became the first African American to cross major-league baseball's color line. Johnny had seen him beat out a bunt, hit an inside-the-park home run, and, most memorably, steal home. Against a backdrop of unyielding pressure his first year up, Robinson batted .297, led the league in stolen bases, and won the Rookie of the Year award. Only later would I come to understand the true significance of Robinson's achievement: the pioneering role he played in the struggle for civil rights, the fact that, after his break-through, nothing would ever be the same—in baseball, in sports, or in the country itself. When I was six it was Robinson, the man, the fiery second baseman, who filled my imagination, taking his huge leads off base, diving headlong to snag a line drive, circling the bases with his strange pigeon-toed gait. "There's no one like him," Johnny said. "He plays to win every minute." "Absolutely," I added, echoing something my father had said. "With nine Jackie Robinsons, we'd never lose a game."

Nothing inspires camaraderie like sharing a victory, not only of a game, but of a season. In the splendid performance of the Dodgers that summer of 1949, my relationship with Johnny flourished. Their opening-day rout of the Giants, 10–3, inspired the demented hope that they would add 153 more wins and history would record the only perfect season in the annals of organized baseball. The experts had predicted that the Dodgers would battle the Cardinals in the National League pennant race. Powered by Stan Musial, Red Schoendienst, and Enos Slaughter, the Cardinals made reality of these prophecies. By the end of June, the two teams stood at the top of the league, chasing one another for first. That month, the Dodgers won nine straight, helped along by Johnny's insistence on wearing the same blue-striped shirt as long as the streak lasted.

After we became friends, I confided in Johnny my understanding that the tower at the entrance to the beach was being used as a prison for bad children. He admitted he had heard the same thing, but he didn't really believe it was true. "Why don't we go over there and find out for ourselves," he suggested. Though I was not really keen on the idea, I didn't want him to know I was afraid, so I followed him to the place where the tower stood. Several times we circled the perimeter of the tower, but there was no sign of life. We were just about to leave when Johnny thought he heard muffled cries coming from inside the structure. I put my ear up against the wall and, sure enough, I heard the same thing. Convinced that it was our job to save the children, we found an indulgent park policeman and led him to the tower. At our insistence, the policeman put his ear against the wall, but said he heard absolutely nothing. When we did the same, the cries we were sure we had heard earlier were no longer audible. We raced back to the pool, determined to try again another day.

Except for Eddie Rust and Steve Bartha, who lived on our block and occasionally joined us girls in punchball, Johnny was the first boy my age that I ever really talked to. On the playground at school, the girls would play on one side, the boys on the other. The boys came over to our side to tug our braids and ponytails, then, cackling, retreated. Being able to talk at length to a boy was something special. And it was my passion for baseball that made it possible.

ON A SULTRY FRIDAY evening that same summer, after months of listening to games on the radio, I saw my first game at Ebbets Field. As my father and I walked up the cobblestone slope of Bedford Avenue and approached the arched windows of the legendary brick stadium, he explained how, as a boy, he had watched the ballpark being built, since the place where he had been sent to live after his parents died was only two blocks away. He was at the site in 1912, when Dodger owner Charles Ebbets pushed a shovel into the ground to begin the excavation. And when the park opened a year later, he was in the bleachers watching the first official game, against the Philadelphia Phillies. He had seen the Dodgers win their first two pennants in 1916 and 1920, only to lose to the Red Sox and the Indians. He had sustained his love affair with "dem Bums" through the frustrating period of the thirties, when the Dodgers were stuck at the bottom of their division, into the happier era of the forties, when under General Manager Branch Rickey they began to look like a championship team. And now my own pilgrimage was about to begin.

The marble rotunda at the entrance to the shrine looked like a train station in a dream, with dozens of gilded ticket windows scattered around the floor. The floor tiles were embellished with baseball stitches, and in the center of the domed ceiling hung an elaborate chandelier composed of a dozen baseball bats. As we started through a tunneled ramp into the stadium, my father told me that I was about to see the most beautiful sight in the world. Just as he finished speaking, there it was: the reddish-brown diamond, the impossibly green grass, the stands so tightly packed with people that not a single empty seat could be seen. I reached over instinctively to hold my father's hand as we wended our way to seats between home plate and first base, which, like the thousands of seats in this tiny, comfortable park, were so close to the playing field that we could hear what the ballplayers said to one another as they ran onto the field and could watch their individual gestures and mannerisms as they loosened up in the on-deck circle. There, come to earth, were the heroes of my imagination, Snider and Robinson and the powerful-looking Don Newcombe; and there were the villains—the "hated New York Giants," an epithet that was to us a single word— Monte Irvin, Sheldon Jones, and the turncoat Leo Durocher.

As the game got under way, my father proceeded to point out to me all the distinguishing features of the park: the uneven right-field wall with the scoreboard in the middle and the Schaefer beer sign on the top, where the "h" would light up for a hit and the "e" for an error; the curious advertisement for Abe Stark's clothing store, "Hit sign, Win suit," which earned Stark such visibility that he was later elected borough president of Brooklyn; the presence of Hilda Chester, a large woman in a print dress repeatedly clanging two cowbells to support the Dodgers and to irritate the opposition; and the arrival of the Sym-Phony, a ragtag band formed by a group of rabid fans whose comic accompaniment had become an institution at Dodger games. When they disagreed with an umpire's call, the little band played "Three Blind Mice." When a strikeout victim from the opposition headed back to the dugout, they played "The Worms Crawl In, the Worms Crawl Out," punctuated by a loud thump on the bass drum as the player sat down on the bench. And when an enemy pitcher was taken out of the game for a reliever, the band serenaded his walk from the mound with "Somebody Else Is Taking My Place." As opposing teams grew increasingly irate at these antics, a sense of camaraderie grew among Dodger fans that made the experience of going to Ebbets Field unforgettable.

I was witness to a splendid first game. Not only did the Dodgers win 4–3, but my hero, Jackie Robinson, ignited the Dodger offense in the second inning when he walked, stole second, went to third on an errant pickoff throw, and scored on an infield out. Watching him on the base path, with his long leads, his feints toward second, and his needling of the pitcher, kept me on the edge of my seat. If he looked awkward when he first started running, with his shoulders rocking and hips swaying, once he gained momentum he created an indelible image. I knew that Jackie's baserunning was part of his mystique, that once he got on base he was such a distraction that the opposing pitcher often lost his concentration and ended up either throwing the ball away trying to pick him off or throwing a bad pitch to the batter at the plate. But to see him in person, through my own eyes instead of Red Barber's, was thrilling. "As long as he got on base," was our ritual refrain, "he was going to do something to bring himself home."

The game at Ebbets Field that day was a first not only for me, but for the sport of baseball as well. When Giant batter Henry Thompson stepped up to bat against Dodger rookie Don Newcombe, it was the first time that a black pitcher faced a black batter in a major-league game. Though Newcombe was the third black player to join the Dodgers after Robinson's debut in 1947 and Campanella's arrival the following year, most of the other teams were slow to follow suit. For the Dodgers, Newcombe's intimidating presence in '49 was critical not only because he became Rookie of the Year but because he provided a certain measure of protection for Robinson. Opposing pitchers knew, if they threw at Robinson, Newcombe would promptly return the favor.

At the start of the '49 season, Branch Rickey had told Robinson that he no longer had to honor the pledge he had made when he first came up, to tolerate insults without retaliation. Freed from this restraint, Robinson was more aggressive than ever at the plate and on the base path, quick to stand his ground against his tormentors. This attitude provoked an even greater desire on the part of opposing pitchers to "get him." Despite the tension on the field, Robinson's newfound freedom proved intensely liberating: the 1949 season would be his best in baseball, earning him the batting title and the MVP award and marking the beginning of six consecutive seasons in which he would hit over .300.

I had brought my red scorebook with me, but it wasn't as easy to concentrate on scoring as it was at home. There was so much to see I wasn't sure where to look. A man two rows behind us had a portable radio with him, and I found myself almost compulsively listening for Red Barber's voice to tell me what I was seeing. Still, I managed to score the entire game, and to this day, I cannot watch a ball game at the ballpark without keeping score. As we left the ballpark, I did not want the evening to end. Sensing this, my father suggested that we stop for ice-cream sodas so that we could go through my scorebook and re-create in full detail the game we had just seen.

I experienced that night what I have experienced many times since: the absolute pleasure that comes from prolonging the winning feeling by reliving the game, first with the scorebook, then with the wrap-up on the radio, and finally, once I learned about printed box scores, with the newspaper accounts the next day. But what I remember most is sitting at Ebbets Field for the first time, with my red scorebook on my lap and my father at my side.

CHAPTER TWO

On summer mornings, my father would come downstairs dressed in his three-piece suit, glance at the gold pocket watch that was attached to his vest with a slender gold chain, kiss my mother and me goodbye, and leave for work. From the window I watched him greet the other men on our block as they walked to the corner to catch the bus for the short ride to the train station, where, every few minutes, an engine whistled, the platform quivered, and one of the seventy-five daily trains swallowed up a new group of commuters for the thirty-eight-minute ride to Penn Station that had made suburban living possible. Now, the fathers departed, our neighborhood, like some newly conquered province, belonged to the women and children.

At my mother's assenting nod, I dashed next door to fetch my best friend, Elaine Friedle, and together we gathered up our gang, upward of a dozen children roughly our age, and began our day's activities. After breakfast, our energy at its height, we raced our bikes down the street, with playing cards clothespinned to the spokes to simulate the sound of a motorcycle, challenging one another to see how many times we could circle the block without holding on to the handlebars. Carelessly discarding bikes on the nearest lawn, skate keys dangling from multicolored lanyards around our necks, we zipped past each other on roller skates, throwing up our hands and shouting in the sheer exuberance of our performance. Then it was on to our endless games of hide-and-seek. My favorite game was ring-a-levio, in which the players on one team would crawl carefully up to the protected circle, hoping to free an imprisoned teammate, and would dart away with a squeal if intercepted by one of the opposing team's guards.

Our days might have seemed shapeless to an adult, but to us, there seemed a definite rhythm to our activities. When we began to tire, we played potsy, a form of hopscotch, on the sidewalk, leisurely jumped rope, rolled marbles, played jacks, or flipped cards against the stoop to see who could come closest to the bottom stair without actually hitting it. After lunch on steamy afternoons when there was no baseball game in progress and no one to take us to the beach, we would jump through the spray of one of the sprinklers which were constantly watering our precious lawns, or lounge on blankets in the shade of a favorite tree for games of Go Fish, Monopoly, and Chinese Checkers.

In the late-afternoon sun, we set up our Kool Aid stands, strategically placed to catch our fathers as they returned in twenty-minute intervals from work, rounding the corners with jackets over their arms as they walked down our street, their faces glistening with sweat, anxious, we thought, for the refreshing drinks we were glad to sell them for the price of a nickel. As my father approached, trying, usually without much success, to maintain a professional demeanor, I would hand him a cup and happily receive the coin he placed in my palm. Soon the summons would come from the front doors of the houses, and we would race in to dinner, not because we were hungry, but in the hope that if we finished quickly enough we could reassemble for another hour or so of play before the encroaching dark put an end to our day on the block.

The small section of Southard Avenue that lay between St. James and Capitolian was my world. Our street, unconnected to any major thoroughfare, and lined by large maple trees which cast a cooling shadow on our activities, was our common land—our playground, our park, our community. If an occasional car passed, we would stand aside, waiting impatiently for the intruder to leave our domain. If we never thought of our neighborhood as safe, that was because it never occurred to us that it could be otherwise—except, of course, for the weed-choked hovel on the corner where the strange and fearsome "Old Mary" lived.

The house in which I grew up was modest in size, situated on less than a tenth of an acre, and separated from the neighboring houses by the narrowest of driveways and a slender strip of grass. For my parents, however, as for other families on the block, the house on Southard Avenue was the realization of a dream. My family had moved to Rockville Centre from the crowded streets of Brooklyn in the late 1930s, early pioneers of that vast postwar migration which was to transform America into a nation of suburbs, and bring to once-bucolic Nassau and Suffolk counties a population as large as that of sixteen of the forty-eight states. Here they would have a single-family home, a private world for themselves and their children, which they could make their own—furnish, repair, remodel—something which only a few years before had seemed the prerogative of the impossibly affluent. They took visible pleasure in every room, the gabled roof, the small enclosed porch that looked out onto the street, the breakfast nook that stood in an alcove off the kitchen, and most of all in the tiny front lawn amid which our house was set. They had land, grass, soil of their own. The great American ambition.

From the front, my house looked narrow and cramped, standing so close to its neighbors that it seemed more like a row house than an independent structure. But on summer nights, when I would lie on the strip of grass that separated us from the Friedles, it seemed to tower above me, its softly lit windows and striped awnings like the side of an ocean liner. My father lovingly tended our lawn as if it were the grounds of an ancestral estate. Every weekend in the summer, he and almost all the fathers could be found outside in their shirtsleeves mowing the small patches of grass, rooting out the occasional weed, planting flowers along the margins of the driveways.

ROCKVILLE CENTRE was home to about eighteen thousand people when I was born, and the population expanded each year until every vacant lot was filled. In contrast to Levittown and other mass-produced suburbs that emerged overnight in the postwar era, our town had been incorporated as a village in the nineteenth century. A century-old Village Hall was set in a green square with a Civil War cannon near the front door. Mature oaks and maples arched over our streets, and our village boasted a variety of housing and a diverse population that many other suburban towns did not enjoy. Old houses mingled with the new: Victorians, Tudors, and Queen Annes stood side by side with newly built split levels and ultramodern ranch houses. The majority of the population was white, as was typical of the suburbs, though more than nine hundred African Americans lived in a neighborhood at the western end of town.

Unlike more affluent modern suburbs, whose fenced homes are encircled by large ornamental lawns, the houses on my block were clustered so close to one another that they functioned

46

almost as a single home. We felt free to dash in to any house for a snack from the mother-in-residence, race through the side door in search of playmates—except for my own house, where my mother's need for tranquillity was respected, making it not only the quietest but sometimes the loneliest house on the block. Since all the families were bringing up children at the same time, babysitters were rarely necessary, for we could usually stay at each other's houses. If one of the mothers was sick, there was always a neighbor or older sister to take her child to school or to the beach. Clothes, bikes, and roller skates were routinely handed down from the older children in one family to the younger ones in another. For me, there was a special benefit in the clustered structure of our block. For the lives within these homes, the stories of each family, formed a body of common lore through which I could expand the compass and vividness of my own life.

The position of our houses determined the pattern of our friendships. Not only did my best friend, Elaine, live next door to me, but her bedroom was directly across the driveway from mine, less than twenty feet away. When we were five, we strung a clothesline between pulleys by our windows and attached a can that allowed us to exchange notes long after our bedtime had passed. When our lights went out, lying on my side facing the open window, barely able to hear my parents talking downstairs, I knew that Elaine was just across the way, in her own bed, facing toward me. Content that everyone was in the proper place, I went to sleep.

Six months older than Elaine and one year ahead of her in school, I learned to read before she did. My mother later told me I had begun deciphering the letters on our soup cans and cereal boxes several months before the day I picked up a book she had read to me many times and read it back to her. Suspecting I had memorized it, she handed me another book to read. I went through it slowly, page by page, reading so loudly that I sounded as if I were addressing an audience of hundreds instead of one. From the moment I read those first paragraphs to my mother, I was obsessed not only with reading but with reading aloud. Everywhere we went, I insisted on reading every sign and billboard along the way. "Why are you doing this?" Elaine asked. "Oh, you'll understand someday," I replied. "Once you start reading, you can never stop."

The books I read filled my imagination, multiplying my daydreams, allowing me to supplement my own collection of stories, previously drawn mostly from my family and my neighbors, with characters and events far removed from the realities of Southard Avenue and Rockville Centre. As I did with the lives of those around me, I could incorporate the people of fiction, even of history, into my own life, make them real, change them, the malleable instruments of my own desire and longing.

I moved from my mother's reading of Kipling's tale about the baby elephant to my own reading of *Little Toot*, the story of the small tugboat with the candy-stick smokestack, who came, as I did, from a family of seamen. When I read about Little Toot's father, Big Toot, the fastest tugboat on the river, and his Grandfather Toot, who breathed smoke and told of mighty deeds, I pictured my uncle Willy and my grandfather Ephraim standing proudly at the helms of their ferryboats, navigating their ships expertly through the tricky currents of the waters surrounding New York and New Jersey. Because all my uncles and grandparents were dead, I had to find some way to keep their memories alive. By fusing what little I knew about their personalities into the characters I liked in the stories I read, I was able to surround myself with the large, vibrant family I always wished I had. And when Little Toot saved the stranded ocean liner and made his family proud, I imagined that someday I would do something that would bring me to the attention of my grandparents in heaven.

Elaine was at least six inches taller than I. I admired her intelligence, and her daring, envied her thick, curly hair and, most of all, her boisterous family. Although most of the houses on the block, including my own, were inhabited by nuclear families, Elaine lived with her brother, mother, father, grand-mother, and great-grandmother—four generations in a single home. On Sundays their house filled with cousins from the city who felt entitled to share in the good fortune and Sunday dinner of the first relatives who had made it to the suburbs.

On Sunday afternoon I would race over to Elaine's house to join the animated conversation and bustle which my own house lacked, to observe as the Friedles and their relatives played Canasta, gambled for pennies, smoked, drank cocktails, listened to music, and danced. I would twirl on the cushioned bar stools in their finished basement, which seemed the height of luxury living, with its large, Formica-topped bar, and watch delightedly as a model train went around the counter and the eyes of a small mechanical man turned red while he raised a drink to his mouth. I listened eagerly to the flow of words, joined in the laughter and chatter, and tried to imagine what it might be like in my own house if I had grandparents, aunts, uncles, cousins, or a mother whose health did not require a placid, less crowded way of life.

The two "old ladies," as we called Elaine's grandmother and great-grandmother, would sit in chairs on the Friedles' front lawn, shouting friendly greetings to the children as we played, telling us stories, gossiping with the neighborhood mothers. The tales they told lured us backward in time to the British colony of Jamaica, in the West Indies, where Elaine's great-grandmother, Amelia, the daughter of Scottish emigrants, was born. Married young, she had eight children, including Elaine's grandmother Valerie, who was widowed shortly after Elaine's mother, Dolly, was born. During the Great War, Amelia's husband left Jamaica to find work in America, promising to send for his family as soon as he was settled. When no word came after six months, Amelia, together with her widowed daughter, Valerie, and her four-year-old-grandIdaughter, Dolly, embarked on a boat for New York to find her husband. After a few fruitless months, they discovered he had moved in with another woman and had no intention of reunion with the family he had left behind. It was not easy for the three women to make it on their own; Elaine's mother, Dolly, could remember slipping on wet urine in the hallway of the New York tenement where she grew up.

Dolly was still in her teens when she met and married George Friedle, a descendant of German immigrants, who had also grown up in a tenement in New York, and whose rapid rise in the world of banking to the position of vice-president of Public National Bank had allowed him, shortly after the Second World War, to move to the suburbs, to his "dream home" on Southard Avenue. And when the family moved to Rockville Centre there was no question but that Dolly's mother and grandmother would accompany them.

The old ladies had brought their folk knowledge with them from Jamaica. When you get married, they instructed Elaine and me, no wedding pictures should be taken, or ghosts will join the ceremony. And on your wedding night, you must keep a set of knives under the bed to ward off the evil spirits. Although we paid careful attention to these strictures, not wanting ghosts or evil spirits at the ceremony which we knew was sure to come, of more pressing concern to six-year-olds was the revelation that three knocks on a door signified death. For some time after being so instructed, I would knock on a friend's door twice, and then stop, trying to gauge how much time had to elapse before the counting could begin again without danger. The precepts were meant to enlighten and amuse, rather than frighten us, for the old ladies were always gentle, with an unerring eye for sadness in a child. If one of us seemed out of sorts, was hurt by our friends, or was left out of a game, they noticed at once and invited us to come into the house to share a bowl of ice cream.

BASEBALL LOYALTIES in our neighborhood were divided between the Yankees, Dodgers, and Giants. As earlier immigrants had brought their ethnic bonds with them to America, the settlers of suburbia had, for the most part, carried their baseball fidelity from their borough of origin—Yankee fans from the Bronx, Giant supporters from Manhattan, and, of course, the devotees of the Dodgers from Brooklyn. In each home, team affiliation was passed on from father to child, with the crucial moments in a team's history repeated like the liturgy of a church service. Over time, each team and its fans had taken on a distinct identity, a kind of stereotype into which the features of the team and the characteristics of its followers were molded to produce an exaggerated caricature. The Yankees were the "Bronx Bombers," whose pinstriped uniforms signified their elite status, supported by the rich and successful, by Wall Street brokers and haughty businessmen. The Dodgers were "dem Bums," the "daffiness boys," the unpretentious clowns, whose fans were seen as scruffy blue-collar workers who spoke with bad diction. The Giants, owned since 1919 by the same family, the Stonehams, were the conservative team whose followers consisted of small businessmen who watched calmly from the stands dressed in shirts and ties, their identity somewhat blurred, caught, as they were, between the Yankee "haves" and the Dodger "have-nots."

To me, however, each team was signified by a member of my small community. The Giants *were* my parents' friends the Goldschmidts, the Rickards down the street, and, most of all, Max Kropf and Joe Schmitt, the butchers around the corner at the Bryn Mawr Meat Market. Loading me down with huge shinbones for my small cocker spaniel, Frosty, they would mock my Dodgers. I would pretend to be angry, but the truth was I loved going into their shop, the feel of the sawdust under my feet as I moved from the muggy August heat into the cooling air of their enormous refrigerator with sides of beef hanging from the ceiling. Most of all, I loved the attention I received, especially when they called me "Ragmop" in honor of my unruly reddish-blond hair. These Giant fans were not dressed in ties and jackets, but wore white aprons, smeared with blood and marrow. Although I tried not to stare, my eyes were often drawn to the rounded stubs of the two fingers Max had cut off while slicing meat. When he caught me looking, he would hold up his hand as if the wound were a badge of honor. "See, Ragmop, this is what happens if you want to be a butcher."

The Yankees were represented by the Friedles, and especially Elaine, who was as devoted to her team as I was to the Dodgers. Since the two teams were in different leagues, our rivalry was muted during the summer months, only to peak again during those frequent Octobers when the Dodgers and the Yankees met in the World Series. She could not understand my idolatry of Jackie Robinson, while I, in turn, heaped scorn on her admiration for the shrill, wiry Billy Martin, the Yankee second baseman known for his quick fists and timely hitting. She would frequently take out her scrapbook of Billy Martin clippings to prove her point—how many hits, his latest batting average, his exploits in the field. How she could compare the tiny, pugnacious Martin to the noble Robinson defied my comprehension. Her enthusiasms and knowledge seemed all the more remarkable since her father, also a Yankee fan, did not encourage her love of baseball, taking her brother, Gary, to games and leaving her at home with the claim that she could never sit through an entire game. Finally, at the age of eight, she exploded in a tantrum of outraged anger, and he agreed to take her, choosing a doubleheader to prove his point. I can still see her look of delight and triumph when she returned to tell me she had loved every minute, and had demanded they stay until the last out of the extra-inning nightcap.

The Yankees also had fervent followers in the Lubars and the Barthas, who lived across the street. Elaine ("Lainie") Lubar's birthday was the day after mine, and her mother would host a joint birthday party to spare my mother the clamorous assemblage of our friends. Only by dint of their cabana at Lido Beach, a symbol of affluence on our block, did the Lubars fit the typical image of the Yankee fan. When Lainie and I went to the beach together, I would race from the car to their family cabana—little more than a concrete hut with striped awnings and deck chairs, but to me, an oasis—where soft drinks were stacked in the refrigerator, and we could sit together for lunch, take a shower after swimming, and put on dry clothes to avoid spending the car ride home in sticky bathing suits on sandy towels.

The most memorable of our neighborhood Yankee fans was Gene Bartha, because of his peculiar dog-walking ritual with Clipper, the family sheepdog. Apparently, Clipper had originally been trained to relieve himself on newspaper in the house, for Gene was obliged to carry a paper with him and intermittently place several sheets on the sidewalk as they walked along. I was walking beside him one night when he mistakenly laid down on the sidewalk the sports page, which had a photograph and lead article on Yogi Berra. Seeing what he had done, he snatched it away from Clipper just in time, deftly replacing the sports page with the front page.

The ultimate aristocrats in the neighborhood—the family with the largest lawn—should, by rights, have been Yankee fans, but the Greenes, like the Rusts and our family, were staunch Dodger fans. The Greenes' home was the only one on our block with a side yard as well as a front yard. I would play with Marilyn, the youngest of their three children, turning cartwheels on their soft grass, lying on my back to divine the shapes of different animals in the clouds, and feeding the rabbits they kept in a hutch on the corner of their lawn. The Rusts' loyalty to the Dodgers followed the more typical pattern. A large Catholic family with five children, the Rusts had carried their allegiance with them when they moved to Long Island from Sheepshead Bay in Brooklyn. And, of course, in Flatbush, my father had literally grown up with Ebbets Field, his devotion to the Dodgers so intertwined with his own biography that my sisters and I could no more have conceived of rooting for another team than of rooting against him.

For all of us, the love was personal and familiar. We spent hours arguing about whether Duke Snider, Willie Mays, or Mickey Mantle was the best center fielder. The handsome, smooth-fielding Duke Snider was the most consistent home-run hitter of the three, but Mays had a balletic grace and a joyful fury, while the switch-hitting Mantle had the greatest raw power and speed. Who was the best announcer: Russ Hodges, Mel Allen, or Red Barber? Who was the better catcher: Roy Campanella, steady behind the plate, unequaled in calling pitches, but a streaky hitter, or the short-armed swarthy Yogi Berra, the most dangerous hitter in baseball in late innings? Was Pee Wee Reese, the "Little Colonel," who held the Dodgers together, a better shortstop than Phil Rizzuto, who led the American League in fielding? And which team had the better double-play combination: the Dodgers with Reese and Robinson, or the Giants with Alvin Dark and Eddie Stanky, whom we called "Eddie Stinky"? For support, we each mustered our own statistics and anecdotes. We carried on our arguments on the street, in the corner stores, and in each other's homes. If no minds were changed, we took great pleasure in our endless debates and our shared love for the sport.

OUR NEIGHBORHOOD LIFE converged on a cluster of stores at the corner of our residential area: the drugstore and butcher shop; the soda shop, which sold papers, magazines, and comics; the delicatessen; and the combination barber shop and beauty parlor. The storekeepers were as much a part of my daily life as the families who lived on my street. When I entered the drugstore for a soda, or went into the delicatessen to buy some potato salad for my mother, the proprietors would greet me by name and, if not occupied, indulge my relentless curiosity. Since the families who operated these stores also owned them, their work was more than a job; it was a way of life. The quality of the goods they sold was as much a manifestation of their pride and self-respect as my father's lawn was to him. The personal services they provided were not motivated merely by a desire for good "customer relations" but by their felt relationship to the larger community which they served and looked upon as neighbors. For our mothers, these neighborhood stores supplied all the goods they needed in the course of an ordinary day, and provided a common meeting place where neighbors could talk, trade advice, and gossip as they relaxed over an ice-cream soda or a cup of coffee.

The sign in St. James Pharmacy, appropriately located on St. James Place, promised "prescription services, reliability, Breyers ice cream, and prompt delivery." But owner "Doc" James Schimmenti gave much more than the advertisement promised. Fastidiously dressed in a white jacket with a white short-sleeved dress shirt, bow tie, and dark pants, Doc was neighborhood nurse and doctor combined. If one of us scraped a knee, he would bandage the cut. If someone got a splinter, he would extract it. When he printed prescription labels, he put his home number on the front so that his customers could call at any hour if they had a question or needed a refill. He was known to deliver as far away as Garden City and as late as 3 A.M. Even on holidays, he was always available. He was so beloved in our neighborhood that we affectionately joked that the store was named for him—St. James—rather than the street on which it stood.

On entering the drugstore, one encountered an old-fashioned soda fountain on the right, with six black stools that twirled around. To the left of the door there were greeting cards and a small bookshelf that held the lending library where my mother rented current bestsellers. On cold winter days, I could come in to warm myself on the grate which heated the store before venturing out again. Two wrought-iron tables with matching chairs were usually occupied by people drinking sodas and waiting for their prescriptions. The shelves held cigarettes and cosmetics; the counter at the center of the store contained a dazzling display of penny candy. In the rear of the store, Doc ground the powders, poured the syrups, and counted pills to fill prescriptions.

Doc, his wife, Josephine, and the four children who made up his close-knit Italian family worked in the store, tending the fountain, unpacking cartons, or operating the register. On nights when the Little League team that

Doc sponsored was playing, the entire family was pressed into action. Doc had promised his players that, whenever they won a game, and they won regularly, he would open the drugstore and treat them all to free ice-cream sodas.

Early one evening, I walked past the store just as the triumphant team was filing in. Doc beckoned me over, and asked me if I might help with the crowd of ballplayers. Unsure of my abilities, but unwilling to miss this splendid opportunity, I walked to the soda fountain with an air of pretended confidence. With Doc guiding me, I pulled the long handle that drew the carbonated water, pushed the short one to add the syrup, and mixed in the cold milk. Finally, with a metal scoop dipped in steamy hot water to soften the hard ice cream, I added two scoops of vanilla or chocolate ice cream and a dab of fresh whipped cream. After the first few sodas, Doc, satisfied, moved away, and I was on my own. My nervous uncertainty drained away as I saw the sodas being swiftly consumed without complaint. I made eighteen sodas that night, handing each one over to one of the boys with a smiling "Here you are," in imitation of Doc Schimmenti himself. When the boys left, I raced home gleefully, holding the dollar I had been given for my work. "And he even paid me," I said to my father that night as I recounted my exploits in soda-by-soda detail.

The butcher shop next to the drugstore, home to my baseball rivals Max and Joe, boasted the best cuts of meat and the freshest vegetables in the entire area. Max, taller and thinner than Joe, was never without his ragged Giant cap as he stooped over the butcher block whistling opera tunes while he cleaved the meat. I was a regular in the store, even when I was only six or seven, for I would do the shopping when my mother wasn't feeling well. Armed with her list, I would watch as they hauled down a huge slab of beef or side of lamb and carried it to the butcher block to be cleaved and cut into steaks, short ribs, or lamb chops. After the meat was cut, they would turn me over to Artie, the vegetable man, who would pick the choicest fruits and vegetables from the display he had made that morning.

When I came in they would often tease me that I had been fast asleep long after their workday had begun. Before dawn, Max would drive to the Bronx Terminal Market, on the Harlem River near Yankee Stadium, to pick out the day's meat and vegetables. "Take me with you," I would beseech him. "Let me see what you're doing while I'm asleep." Finally, he agreed, discussed it with my mother and one Saturday morning, picked me up in his truck just before three. My mother had furnished fresh coffee cake, which we devoured as we made our way into the Bronx. Perched on the high front seat next to Max, I began my customary interrogation. Had he always wanted to be a butcher, how had he gotten started, where had he come from? He told me he had arrived in the United States from Germany during the Depression, sponsored by his uncle Ottoman in New York. When he reached the city, however, things were so difficult that his uncle had no work for him. He saw an ad for a position in a North Shore butcher shop and walked twenty-five miles to Long Island to ask for the job. Though he knew nothing about cutting meat, he persuaded the owner to take a chance. Eventually, they became partners. From that shop, he moved to the store in Rockville Centre.

It was almost 4 A.M. as we approached the sprawling labyrinth of the Bronx Terminal, then the largest wholesale food market in the world, occupying thirty-two acres, stretching from 149th Street to 152nd Street and called a "terminal" market because it was the end of the line for runs from farms to the city. Although it was still pitch-black when we pulled up to the long brick warehouses, there were so many people gathered around the illuminated counters that it seemed like midday. Fruits, lettuce, celery, and broccoli were displayed in wood-and-wire slotted crates, which were discarded as they emptied. Kids would come at day's end, lug off the discarded crates, and, with old roller skates, fashion homemade scooters. Firmly clasping Max's hand, I walked with him for nearly an hour as he picked out what he wanted, and then stood beside him as he loaded it into the back of the truck. Soon we were back on the road, heading east toward home, just in time to see my first sunrise.

For me, each store was a treasure house of lore about the varied lives of the people of my community. I marveled that for Carl and Edna Probst, the husband-and-wife team who ran the delicatessen, unlike my own parents, there was no separation of the workplace and the living place, no division which forced the woman to stay home with the children and the man to spend his working day in the city, away from his family, his leisure time away from his place of work. I imagined that when I grew up I would enjoy a similar marriage—my husband and I would work side by side, day after day, waiting on people, making potato salad, and slicing cold cuts.

Whenever I entered the delicatessen I was greeted by the blended odors of good cheese, cold cuts, and pickles. In contrast to the neon lights and wide corridors of modern supermarkets, the delicatessen was small and narrow, with dark wooden shelves that resembled library stacks, packed from floor to ceiling with colorful cans instead of books. Because the shelves were so high, long-handled clippers were needed to reach the hard-to-get items. When the store was not crowded, Edna and Carl let me manipulate the clippers myself, positioning the arms around a box of cereal or a can of Campbell's soup, squeezing the grip to tighten the clippers, and then lowering the container to a point where it could drop into my arms.

One Thanksgiving when my mother was in the hospital, Edna and Carl invited our family to join them for dinner. Since they had decided to stay open in case any of their customers needed something at the last minute, they celebrated in the back of the store, setting out dinner at the big table where each morning they made the tuna and potato salads. When I walked through the decorated cloth curtain which separated the front of the store from the back, I was excited to find this back room as warm and personal as a home; a large wood stove and a small maple table made it cozy, as a kitchen should be on a cold Thanksgiving day.

The owners of the soda shop next door were not quite as friendly. We were convinced that Mr. and Mrs. Brand hated us. Mrs. Brand was short and fat, with bleached-blond hair and beady eyes. If we took too long in the comics section without buying anything, Mr. Brand, with hair like Brillo, took delight in kicking us out of the store. Their attitude brought out the worst in us. Over and over, we would call the store and ask in disguised voices if they had "Prince Albert in the can." When they confirmed it, we would start laughing and say, "'Well, please let him out. He deserves to be free!" For maximum satisfaction one of us would be stationed in the store during the calls to watch Mrs. Brand screw up her prune-like face in anger at the third Prince Albert inquiry and retort, "No, we won't let him out, but if we catch you, we'll put *you* in the can!"

Nevertheless, the Brands made the best

sodas in town, boasting more flavors than Howard Johnson's, and their booths were large and comfortable. They had a son, Eddie, who also worked in the store. He always wore a bow tie, and we sensed that he wanted to be nice to us but was afraid to let his guard down when his parents were there.

I WAS ONLY two years old when the end of World War II signaled the often involuntary return of women to the homes they had left for the factories and shipyards of wartime America. The re-entry of millions of men into the work force, together with pervasive fear of a return to large-scale unemployment, was fertile ground for the growth of an ideology which sought to persuade women that work and education would destroy their chances for marriage and a happy home life. The media and pundits of the day instructed women that their only true fulfillment could be found as wives and mothers, that sexist discrimination was actually good for them, that the denial of opportunity was, in reality, the manifestation of the highest possible goals of womanhood. The president of Mills College argued that higher education could actually be harmful for women, since the total irrelevance of their studies to their destined roles as wives and mothers would only increase their frustration. If Rosie the Riveter, women pilots, and Women's Army Corps members had been portrayed as the heroines of the forties, the heroines in the fifties were women who were wise enough to realize that work and marriage were incompatible and had renounced careers to raise a family. This reassertion of dying values worked, at least for a while. Women valedictorians who left the commencement stage to become suburban housewives were praised as paragons of femininity. A renowned concert pianist, Liz Eck, became a media darling, a credit to her gender, for her decision to leave the stage in order to tend her husband and mother her child. Grace Kelly gave up her dazzling Hollywood career to become a wife and mother, albeit with a principality thrown into the bargain. In *Life* magazine in the mid-fifties, Robert Couglan railed against "the disease of working women," who insisted on ruining their children and their family life.

If my mother felt a conflict of desire between her own ambitions and her family, she never showed it to me. On the contrary, she took great pride in being a housewife and seemed to enjoy her inviolable routine. On Mondays and Wednesdays, Frank, the Dugan's Bakery man, came with fresh bread, coffee cake, and cupcakes; on Tuesdays and Thursdays, the milkman, whose name was Ray, arrived at the back door with glass bottles of Evans' milk, which came with a layer of cream on the top that had to be scooped out with a special spoon. On Fridays, the chime of a bell signaled the arrival of the iceman, with large rectangular chunks of ice held between sharp metal tongs; a second bell heralded the man who sharpened knives and scissors, the sparks flying from the grindstone against which he held the blade. We had a Monitor refrigerator in our pantry, a Bendix washer in the basement, and a pentagonal clothesline in the backyard where our clothes were hung out to dry. My mother presided over the myriad details of life, deftly orchestrating the well-being of our household to the rhythm of the seasons: storm windows went up and down, slipcovers were put on and taken off, winter clothes were stored with mothballs, summer rugs replaced winter rugs, and the awnings were put up and removed.

Because she was such a methodical housekeeper, my mother had plenty of time to read her beloved books, walk to the corner stores, or visit with neighbors. I never sensed that she was bored or lonely. She always took special pains to put on fresh lipstick and to comb her hair when she knew that my father was on his way home. As soon as she saw him coming down the street, she began preparing the Manhattan cocktails which they shared every single night of their married life as they sat together on our porch and talked about their day. She seemed to grow more vibrant as they talked, asking him questions about work, and listening with unwavering interest and sympathetic understanding. He in turn asked her what she had done, whom she had talked with, and what she had read. When, occasionally, I listened to them talk, I could sense their love for one another, which made me happy, though I felt jealously excluded from their conversation. Indeed, so special was their ritual cocktail hour that my father never drank another Manhattan after my mother's death.

These repetitive days seemed fulfilling for my mother. But I could never be sure. I was unable to share her interior life as she shared mine, a barrier strengthened, I suspect, by her illness. She must have known that her heart was growing weaker each year and worried about how much longer she would live. Not wanting me to know her fears, she rarely talked about her illness, never revealing to me what must have been a continual preoccupation. Yet, despite the weakness and fragility of her body, my mother stamped her personality in every alcove and corner of every room.

For as far back as I can remember, she was the overseer of some project in our house: a change of wallpaper in the bedroom, new paint in the kitchen, a new slipcover for the couch in the living room. My father was the work force for all these projects: painting the walls, hanging the wallpaper, and building the rock garden that my mother planted. After working with figures all week long, he relaxed on the weekends by working with his hands, and took pride in the tools he had assembled over the years. We used to tease our parents that when they both got to heaven we could expect that the sky would be a different color each day, with Mother giving orders and Dad doing the painting.

For the most part, I was little more than an

eager witness and cheerleader for these activities. One summer, however, when I was about six, my father rented a steamer to take the old wallpaper off the dining-room wall. Intrigued by this strange machine, I volunteered my services, and then, when my suggestion met little enthusiasm, I pleaded for a chance to try it. Reluctantly, my father gave me the steamer, and with a little yelp of enthusiasm, I proceeded to strip off the thermostat, to the stunned merriment of my father. The only housework I ever enjoyed was on the nights my father designated me the person to put away the dishes he had dried. While I stood by the cabinets, he threw the plates and the silverware across the room to my waiting hands. Though we lost a few dishes along the way, my father had managed to transform an otherwise tedious chore into a great adventure.

Every year, my parents had more money to spend, a prosperity shared by almost everyone in the neighborhood. Excitement infected the entire block when someone got a new refrigerator with a built-in freezer, an automatic washing machine, or a television set with a bigger screen. Critics have railed against the acquisitiveness of the fifties generation, but for our parents, who had lived through the Depression, the ever-expanding economy seemed like a miraculous cornucopia; they took nothing for granted, and approached each major purchase with a sense of awe.

THE SOLITARY EXCEPTION to the genteel circumstances of middle-class life in our neighborhood was the old woman who lived in the run-down wooden shack with peeling paint on the corner of our street, known to us only as Old Mary. She was dressed always in black, and she had only one leg. The tapping of her wooden stump as she hobbled down the street, muttering, her body hunched, her eyelids half closed, terrified the children of the block and sent us scurrying for cover. A look of anger invariably darkened her creased face, and her hands seemed to make vague menacing gestures.

Old Mary was the "bad witch" of our neighborhood, something straight out of the fairy tales we read. As we rounded her corner, we would retreat to the safety of the opposite curb and spy on her, trying to decipher her movements while we watched her dig threatening holes in the ground behind her shack. Our vision obscured by the tangle of weeds, raspberry canes, and briar that surrounded her property, we imagined that she was making those holes to dispose of children she had kidnapped and killed. Through one of her windows we thought we spied the outline of a skull, which we believed she had placed there as a warning.

We fed on our own fear, daring one another to dash into her yard and peer directly into her windows. A glimpse of the inside of her house would, we believed, provide evidence of her witchcraft. For each of these escapades we concocted military-style stratagems. One or two lookouts would back up the brave person who volunteered to make the run, ready to sound a warning at the first sight of Old Mary. No one was eager to do the job, but one summer day Eddie Rust finally volunteered. After swiftly crossing the street, he darted through the jungle of canes and weeds and had just reached the window of her shack when Old Mary suddenly appeared. She caught Eddie by the back of his belt, her face twisted in anger, her screams chilling even at our distance of twenty feet. For several very long seconds, we stood frozen on the sidewalk, before Eddie struggled free and we raced off down the street. She began chasing us with what seemed supernatural endurance for an old lady. Though our houses promised sanctuary, we were afraid to have her know where we lived, so we ran in the opposite direction. Every time we glanced back, she was there, the staccato thump of her wooden leg on the sidewalk amplified in our frightened brains. Long after we eluded her, we couldn't stop shaking.

A few days later, I bounded down our front steps to find my mother standing on the sidewalk talking to Old Mary herself. I turned immediately to escape back into the house, but my mother's voice aborted my flight. Beckoning me over with a smile, she presented me to Old Mary and waited expectantly for me to say hello. Eyes cast downward, my voice muffled, I managed a pathetic semblance of a greeting. My mother's solicitous expression and friendly voice betrayed a disquieting familiarity as I listened to her inquire after Mary's health. Mary asked my mother a question about her flowers, and in response my mother led her through our driveway to show her something in the rock garden at the back of our house. As I stood there transfixed, watching them walk alongside the house, I imagined that my mother pointed to my bedroom window. Now that Old Mary knew where I slept, there was nothing to prevent her from flying through my window during the night and spiriting me away.

While I was getting ready for bed, my mother came up to my room, and in a tone devoid of sympathy said, "I don't understand what you're so afraid of." I felt trapped between the fearsome realities of Old Mary and my mother's accusing tone. I did my best to relate how she had yelled at us and then chased us down the road. "And what provoked her to do this?" my mother asked. "I have no idea," I said, shrugging my shoulders. "Is it possible that you were on her property and trampled her flowers?" "I never did," I replied, stressing the "I" so that my response was not completely untrue.

Sternly, she told me that my behavior was unacceptable, that Mary was simply a poor, sick old woman who had come from the Ukraine and had never learned to speak English very well. In fact, my mother explained, she had lived on our block longer than all the rest of us. Originally, her house stood in the midst of the vacant lots on which all the other houses were eventually built. Even some of the adults, she admitted, complained about the condition of Mary's house and the weeds that violated the rules of the game in the suburbs. "Age and poverty are not a sin," she said. Unconvinced, I rejoined feebly that all the other kids felt the same way, which only further irritated her. That night, I couldn't sleep; every shadow looked like a witch's broom.

"I am going to visit Mary, and you're coming with me," my mother announced as I entered the kitchen for breakfast the next morning. I tried to protest, but her tone brooked no argument, so I followed her out of the house and down the block. As we approached the dirt path which led through the weeds to Mary's door, I alternated between closing my eyes as a kind of protection, and observing every detail so that if I got out alive I would have a great tale to tell. We passed through the outer tangle of weeds that surrounded the house like a palisade, and I was stunned to see a magnificent garden. The place was a wilderness of gold and purple and violet. There were marigolds, giant zinnias, and daylilies, and a rosebush climbing up the walls of her shack filled the air with perfume. Now I realized what she was doing as we watched her stooped and digging in her yard.

When she came to her door in response to my mother's knock that morning, Old Mary didn't seem quite so hideous and menacing as before. Quickly, I glanced inside. There were no rugs or couches. Her cabin was dark and unpleasant. My eyes scanned the room for the skull we had seen through the window, long a fixture of our fantasies. It didn't take long to find—a mannequin's head, decked in a wig, was placed on the counter in front of the window. I turned back to look at the intricately patterned garden and suddenly realized why someone crashing in and trampling upon her flowers was so threatening to her. Our feared witch was simply a reclusive old lady, a remnant from another time and culture, minding her own business and cultivating a beautiful garden.

Two months later, Old Mary died. When the police came to her house, they found several hundred thousand dollars in cash hidden beneath some boards behind her toilet. No one ever figured out where the cash had come from, or why Mary had not used it to make her life easier. In short order, the bulldozers came and razed Old Mary's shack, erasing the last visible reminder of the poverty from which all our families had escaped.

MY FIRST YEAR as a Dodger fan ended with a dramatic flourish as the pennant race between the Dodgers and the Cardinals came down to the final week. On September 21, 1949, with the Cardinals a game and a half ahead, the Dodgers arrived in St. Louis for a three-game series, including a day-night doubleheader. Second grade forced me to miss most of the first game, but I arrived home in time to hear the

Cardinals, sparked by Enos Slaughter, rally in the bottom of the ninth to break a scoreless tie and win the game. Fortunately, the tide began to turn in the second game: Preacher Roe, so skinny that he looked like the schoolmaster Ichabod Crane, pitched a shutout to beat the Cards 5–0. The Dodgers convincingly won the third game with nineteen runs and nineteen hits, the kind of lopsided victory which delighted me far more than a tension-filled pitching duel. Trailing now by only half a game, the Dodgers went on to split a series with the Phillies and win two from the Braves. The two teams entered the last game of the season with the Dodgers on top by one. A Dodger victory would win the pennant, a loss would force a playoff.

I listened with both my parents to the final game, which took place on a Sunday afternoon at Shibe Park in Philadelphia. The Dodgers scored five runs in the third, but, by the bottom of the ninth, the Phillies had bounced back to tie the game at seven apiece. I couldn't sit still. My throat felt so dry that it hurt, but I was afraid to leave the room. "Now you're learning what it means to be a Dodger fan," my father said. Then, in the top of the tenth, Pee Wee Reese opened with a single, which was followed by two more singles to score two runs, and the Dodgers held on to win the pennant. My father hoisted me up and twirled me around and told me that I was the good-luck charm that brought victory to our team. And so I believed I was.

Soon it seemed that everyone on our block had emptied into the street, laughing and joking and sharing the moment, for that Sunday marked a double victory for New York fans. Thirty minutes before the Dodgers won, the Yankees had clinched the American League pennant with an equally dramatic win over the Boston Red Sox. The Sox and the Yanks had come to the last day of the season tied for first, with identical records: the winner of the last game would win the pennant. Not since 1908 had pennant races in both leagues come down to the last day. New York took a 5–0 lead into the ninth, when the Sox rallied for three runs, but the Yankees held on to win their sixteenth and perhaps most hard-won pennant, since time and again in the course of the season they had come back from adversity, plagued by more than seventy-one major injuries, including the loss of Joe DiMaggio for half their games. In a moment of joyful truce, before we hardened into our partisan camps, prepared to collide once again in the World Series, Elaine and I hugged each other. Mr. Lubar and my father shook hands, Mr. Rust, Eileen and Eddie Rust's father, patted Gene Bartha on the back.

After the spectacular pennant drive, the '49 World Series proved anticlimactic. The Yankees took the first game when Tommy Henrich hit a solo homer in the ninth inning to break a scoreless pitching duel between Allie Reynolds and Don Newcombe. The Dodgers returned the favor in the second game with a 1–0 victory by Preacher Roe. After two such close games, however, the Yankees won the next three straight. Our dreams for a world championship in '49 withered and died. My relationship with Elaine grew strained and suffered for weeks. It was that October that I first understood the pain, bravado, and prayer woven into the simple slogan that served Dodger fans as a recurring anthem: "Wait till next year."

CHAPTER THREE

My early years were happily governed by the dual calendars of the Brooklyn Dodgers and the Catholic Church. The final out of the last game of the World Series signaled the approach of winter, bringing baseball hibernation, relieved only by rumors of trades and reports of contract negotiations. Even before the buds had appeared on the trees of Rockville Centre, players had sloughed off their winter weight and prepared to reconvene for spring training, bringing the joyous return of the box score (whose existence my father had finally revealed). Excitement mounted as the team returned to Brooklyn for opening day, a day of limitless promise. As spring yielded to summer, the pennant race began to heat up, reaching a peak of intensity— of mingled hope and apprehension—during the sultry days of August, when the hopes of many teams were still alive. By mid-September, a chill in the air of shortening days, the scales began to tip, depressing the hopes of many teams. For fans of contending teams, however, like the Dodgers of my childhood, it was Indian summer, a glorious respite before the last out of the last game opened the door once more to winter.

Analogous to the seasonal cycles of baseball were the great festivals of the Catholic Church. A month before Christmas we hung the Advent wreath, and each week we lit one of the four candles that presaged the coming of the Christ child. The fulfillment of Christmas followed, symbolized by the decoration of our Christmas tree, the exchange of gifts, and the mystery and wonder of Midnight Mass. When I was five or six, I would lie awake in bed, listening as the thunder of church bells at midnight announced the coming of the Savior, and dream of the day I would be permitted to stay up late enough to accompany my sisters to Midnight Mass. When I was finally allowed to go, none of my imaginings prepared me for the splendor of the church, its marble altars bordered with garlands of white and red poinsettias and dotted with red flames from clusters of small white candles surrounding the central one that symbolized Christ, the Light of the World. My parents worried that I wouldn't last through the two-hour service, but the sight of the altar, the priests' gold vestments, the sounds of the Latin ritual, and the soaring choir music overwhelmed fatigue until long after the service was completed.

The last weeks of winter brought Ash Wednesday and the beginning of Lent, commemorating the period of Jesus' fast in the desert. We knelt before the priest, who traced in ash the sign of the cross on our foreheads. "Remember," the priest intoned, his thumb touching each brow, "that thou art dust and unto dust shalt thou return." How much nearer death seemed to me when I was a child, when, kneeling like millions of other children, I said the nightly prayer: "Now I lay me down to sleep, I pray the Lord my soul to keep. If I should die before I wake, I pray the Lord my soul to take." But symbols of death were more than matched by symbols of rebirth, renewal, and resurrection, as the Lenten feast led up to Palm Sunday, marking the triumphal return of Jesus to Jerusalem. Holy Week—windows opening to the onrushing spring—continued through the solemnity of Holy Thursday and the deep mourning of Good Friday, when the church stood desolate and bare, its altar draped in black, its statues covered in purple, giving way to the joyful triumph of Easter Mass, when the church was bedecked in white lilies. As Easter had been preceded by forty days of sorrow, it was followed by fifty days of rejoicing, leading up to Whitsunday, the feast of the Pentecost, and the gift of the Holy Spirit. Through these seasonal festivals, so firmly embedded in the routine of our lives,

I developed a lasting appreciation of the role that pageantry, ritual, and symbolism play in tying together the past and the present.

I took great pride in the commanding beauty of my church, St. Agnes. Built in the thirties to resemble a fifteenth-century Gothic cathedral, St. Agnes was furnished with oak pews that could seat over twelve hundred people. Its luminous windows made of antique stained glass had been imported from England and Germany, and its bell tower, surmounted by an aluminum cross, was visible for miles. I regarded with awe the serene darkness of the interior, a vast clear space illuminated by the soft amber light of two dozen iron chandeliers, hanging in two rows on long chains from the vaulted ceiling. Like something out of the Arthurian Legend, richly colored banners honoring the saints were mounted on lines of decorated poles projected from the side walls. These colorful lines converged at the sanctuary, with its white marble altar and its enormous crucifix suspended on chains from the canopy.

The scale of the church was the result of the vision of one man, Father Peter Quealy. He had arrived in Rockville Centre at the turn of the century, only two decades after six families had organized a tiny Roman Catholic parish and celebrated Mass in a blacksmith's shop. Under Father Quealy's inspired guidance, the pastorate increased to hundreds and then thousands, outgrowing two churches until the present St. Agnes was built, covering an entire block in the center of the village, with the church, rectory, convent, and a parochial school. When the foundation was laid in 1935, many thought Father Quealy's reach had exceeded his grasp, but in 1957 the church built on the scale of a cathedral actually became a cathedral: Pius XII announced that a new Catholic diocese, encompassing Nassau and Suffolk counties on Long Island, was to be formed out of the existing Brooklyn Diocese, with St. Agnes Church as its seat. By then Father Quealy's health was failing, but he lived to witness the celebratory Mass, attended by six hundred priests, one hundred monsignori, three archbishops, twenty-five bishops, and nine hundred nuns, at which Bishop Walter Kellenberg assumed the throne and officially made St. Agnes a cathedral.

WHEN I WAS SEVEN years old, my twin passions for the church and baseball collided. It was 1950, the year of my First Holy Communion. Every Wednesday afternoon at two-thirty, all Catholics who attended second grade in public school, as I did, were released early to attend the classes at St. Agnes that would prepare us for First Communion, admitting us into the congregation of the Catholic Church. Whereas the parochial-school students were allowed to receive their First Communion in the first grade, the rest of us had to wait an extra year, so that the nuns could compensate for all the rigorous hours of instruction that were lost. Our class was held in a dark room in the parochial school, the large map of the forty-eight states that adorned the back wall of our public-school room supplanted by a gallery of the saints. There was the infant St. Ambrose, on whose mouth a swarm of bees had settled, causing his elders to predict great oratorical gifts; St. Patrick, the apostle of Ireland, brandishing a staff as he expelled the serpent of sin and paganism from Ireland. My favorite saint was the Jesuit, Aloysius Gonzaga, the patron of youth, whose name my father had taken at his own confirmation, completing the full name I loved to say aloud—Michael Francis Aloysius Kearns.

Our teacher, Sister Marian, was a small Dominican nun who seemed ancient at the time but was probably in her fifties, with a gentle manner, a flowing white habit with a wimple pulled so tight her forehead was stretched smooth, and cheeks that bore such deep lines that the bottom and top of her face appeared the composite of two different people. Sister Marian introduced us to the text familiar to generations of Catholic schoolchildren: the blue-covered Baltimore Catechism with a silver Mary embossed on a constellation of silver stars. The catechism was organized around a series of questions and answers we had to memorize word for word to help us understand the meaning of what Christ had taught and, ultimately, to understand Christ Himself. "Who made us? God made us." "Who is God? God is the Supreme Being who made all things."

"Why did God make us? God made us to show forth His goodness and to share with us His everlasting happiness in heaven." Although it was learned by rote, there was something uniquely satisfying about reciting both the questions and the answers. No matter how many questions we had to memorize, each question had a proper answer. The Catholic world was a stable place with an unambiguous line of authority and an absolute knowledge of right and wrong.

We learned to distinguish venial sins, which displeased our Lord, from the far more serious mortal sins, which took away the life of the soul. We memorized the three things that made a sin mortal: the thought or deed had to be grievously wrong; the sinner had to know it was grievously wrong; and the sinner had to consent fully to it. Clearly, King Herod had committed a mortal sin when, intending to kill the Messiah, he killed all the boys in Judea who were two years old or less. Lest we feel too far removed from such a horrendous deed, we were told that those who committed venial sins without remorse when they were young would grow up to commit much larger sins, losing their souls in the same way that Herod did.

Every Tuesday night, the day before my class in religious instruction, my mother would drill me on the weekly lesson. She never betrayed the slightest impatience, and she made it fun by playing games with me. She held up playing cards numbered one through seven for the seven gifts of the Holy Ghost—wisdom, understanding, counsel, fortitude, knowledge, piety, and fear of the Lord—placing the appropriate card on the table as I recalled each one. In similar fashion, I learned the three theological virtues, the ten commandments, and the seven sacraments. And when I had to memorize various prayers—the Our Father, the Hail Mary, and the Apostles' Creed—she put a glass of milk and a box of Oreo cookies on the table so I could savor my success at the completion of each prayer.

In class, Sister Marian explored each commandment with us in fuller detail. To understand the eighth commandment—"Thou shalt not bear false witness against thy neighbor"—we were told to imagine emptying a feather pillow from the roof of our house, then trying to pick up every feather. If it seemed impossible for us to imagine gathering all the feathers back into the pillow, Sister explained, "so would you never be able to get the rumor you told about someone back from everyone who heard it."

My imagination was kindled by the concept of baptism. We learned that we were all born with souls that were dead in original sin under the power of the devil, but that baptism gave us new life and freed us from Satan's grasp. Without baptism, one could not receive any of the other sacraments or go to heaven. The part that particularly aroused me, however, was the thought that, if an unbaptized person was dying, and no priest was present, it was up to us—i.e., me— to perform the sacrament by pouring ordinary water on the forehead of the dying person and saying aloud: "I baptize thee in the name of the Father, and of the Son, and of the Holy Ghost." More than once, I used my unbaptized doll to practice the sacrament of baptism. I would make her comfortable on my pillow, run into the bathroom directly across the hall, fill a plastic cup with water, and very solemnly launch her toward salvation.

Sister Marian told us stories about the early Christian martyrs who were willing, sometimes even eager, to die for their faith when put to the test by the evil Roman emperor, Nero. After a great fire destroyed much of Rome six decades after Christ, Nero's people began to suspect that he had started the fire himself to clear a site for his proposed "Golden House" and had celebrated the conflagration on his fiddle. To deflect the people's wrath, he made the Christians of Rome his scapegoats, sending them into the jaws of lions if they insisted on professing their Christian faith. Many a night I lay awake worrying whether I might lack courage to die for my faith, fearing that when the test came I would choose instead to live. Lions began populating my dreams, until visits to the Bronx Zoo found me standing in front of the lion's cage, whispering frantically to the somnolent, tawny beast behind the bars in hopes that, if ever I were sent as a martyr to the lions' den, my new friend would testify to his fellow lions that I was a good person. Evading the terrible choice, I could exhibit courage, affirm my faith, and still manage to survive.

So RICH WERE the traditions and the liturgy of my church that I could not imagine being anything other than Catholic. Though there were Jews and Protestants on our block—the Lubars and the Barthas were Jewish, the Friedles and the Greenes Protestant—I knew almost nothing about these other religions. I could not describe what distinguished an Orthodox Jew from a Reform Jew, or say what made someone a Methodist rather than a Presbyterian or Episcopalian. I understood that our neighbors were devoted to their religions, lighting Sabbath candles on Friday or attending services Saturday or Sunday. Their church or synagogue was central to their social lives. The Friedles were very active in the Mr. and Mrs. Club at the Congregational church, which sponsored dances, pot-luck dinners, and card-playing evenings, and their children attended Sunday school every week. I knew that the Lubars were active in their temple and that the Greenes, who had been the Greenbergs before converting to Protestantism, were equally involved in their church. Indeed, in my neighborhood, everyone seemed to be deeply involved in one religion or another. Although I observed the fellowship that other religions provided, I had no inkling of what beliefs they inculcated in their followers. We were taught only that these people were non-Catholics and that we should not read their literature or inquire about their beliefs. Furthermore, it was, we thought, a grievous sin for us to set foot in one of their churches or synagogues.

It was this last admonition that produced my first spiritual crisis. In early February 1950, our newspaper, the *Long Island News and Owl,* reported that Dodger catcher Roy Campanella was coming to Rockville Centre. He planned to speak at a benefit for the local black church, then under construction, the Shiloh Baptist Church. The program was to be held in the Church of the Ascension, an Episcopal church one block from St. Agnes.

The son of an Italian American father and an African American mother, Campanella had joined the Baltimore Elite Giants, one of the great teams in the Negro League, when he was only fifteen. In short order, his skill in calling pitches, his ability to fathom the vulnerability of an opposing hitter, his strong arm, his prowess at the plate, and his endurance became legendary. He once caught four games in a single day: a twin bill in Cincinnati on a Sunday afternoon, followed by a bus ride to Middletown, Ohio, and another doubleheader that evening. Unlike Jackie Robinson, who considered his experience in the Negro League demeaning, Campanella claimed to have thoroughly enjoyed his years in black baseball. Less combative and more conciliatory than

Robinson, Campanella repeatedly said that he thought of himself as a ballplayer, not a pioneer; that, when he was catching or hitting, he focused only on what the pitcher was throwing, not the color of his opponent. Since his rookie season with the Dodgers in 1948, he had established himself unequivocally as the best catcher in the National League. In 1949 he led all catchers with a .287 batting average, twenty-two doubles, and twenty-two home runs.

I couldn't wait to tell my father that his favorite player would be coming to our town, so he would get tickets and take me with him. I begged my mother to take me to the train station so I could tell my father the dramatic news as soon as he stepped off the platform. As our car passed St. Agnes on the way to the station, however, it dawned on me that Campanella was scheduled to speak in the *Episcopal* church. "Oh, no!" I said. "It can't be." "What?" my mother asked. Close to tears, I announced that there was no hope of my going after all, since I was forbidden to set foot in the Episcopal church. Campanella was coming to my town and I could not even go to see him. To my surprise, my mother simply said, "Well, let's see, let's wait and talk to Daddy." When I explained the dilemma to my father, he said that he understood the church's prohibition against participating in the service of another church, but he didn't really believe it extended to attending a lecture by a baseball player in the parish hall. He was certain it would be proper for us to go and would get the tickets the following day.

Reassured, I put my qualms aside until the big night arrived and the moment came to cross the threshold of the white clapboard church. A sudden terror took possession of me, and my knees began to tremble. Fearing that we would be struck dead in retaliation for our act of defiance, I squeezed my body against my father and let his momentum carry me past the door, through the sanctuary, and into the parish hall. At first, I tried to keep my eyes on the ground, but I soon found myself surveying the simple altar, small windows, and plain wooden pews, so much less ornate and imposing than ours. A podium had been set up in the hall with about 150 folding chairs, and we were lucky enough to find seats in the second row.

The program opened with choral singing, which subsided as the black Baptist minister, Reverend Morgan Days, came forward to introduce the squat, powerful Campanella, dressed in a black shirt and a light jacket with broad lapels. His topic was not baseball, but "Delinquency and Sportsmanship." Nonetheless, I tried to absorb every word. Children, he argued, were not born with prejudice but were infected with it by their elders. The only way to combat this cycle of bigotry was to bring kids of different races together early on in social and recreational programs. He had a surprisingly squeaky voice for a powerful looking man, but his message rang with such conviction that he received a standing ovation. When his presentation ended, Campanella stood around for half an hour shaking hands with everyone. There were a dozen things I wanted to say, but when he turned and took my hand, I managed only to thank him for being a Dodger and for coming to our town. The warmth of his broad smile was all I needed to know that this was a night I would never forget.

My earlier fear returned, however, as I climbed into bed that night. The warnings of the nuns tumbled through my head, convincing me that I had traded the life of my everlasting soul for the joy of one glorious night when I held Roy Campanella's strong hand in a forbidden church. Jumping out of bed, I got down on my knees and repeated every prayer I could remember, in the hope that each would wipe away part of the stain that the Episcopal church had left on my soul. I was distracted in school the following day, and again that night had difficulty falling asleep. It was a Friday night, and my parents were playing bridge with three other couples in the dining room, so I could not run downstairs and curl up on the porch sofa, as I sometimes did when I could not fall asleep.

I must have dozed off, because the long-drawn-out squeal of a siren awakened me. Three times the siren wailed, paused, then started again, summoning members of the volunteer fire department. I ran downstairs to find my worried parents and their friends.

"They're calling *all* the surrounding towns!" my father exclaimed, listening to the pattern of the alarm. "Not just Rockville Centre," said my mother. At that moment, my sister Jeanne ran into the house with her friends. "There's been an awful train wreck!" she announced, breathless. "Two trains—it's gruesome!" Shaking, she burst into tears. We found out from her friends that they had followed the crowd to the station after a basketball game at the high school, but the scene was so appalling that they had to turn around and come home. My parents and their friends debated whether they should go into town; I remember my mother remarking that it was ghoulish to be a spectator to misery and unable to do anything about it.

As I eavesdropped, I began to discern in this calamity an opportunity for my own redemption. If there were no priests present, if I could locate a dying person and baptize him "in the name of the Father, and of the Son, and of the Holy Ghost," thus granting his entrance to heaven, I would earn considerable points toward purging my sin. I grabbed my coat and slipped undetected out the front door while my parents were still absorbed by the catastrophic news. Although it was cold and dark, I wasn't afraid as I set forth on the familiar route to my grammar school, knowing the train station was in the same direction. Once I rounded the corner at Brower, the pitch-darkness scared me and I considered returning home, but just then one of my sister's friends offered me a ride, and soon we were joined by hundreds of people, all moving in the same direction. Emergency floodlights and car headlights leached the color from faces as the crowd surged forward. My heart hammered with excitement. I was ready. Though I had no water to pour on the forehead of my convert, I figured I could find some clean snow that would serve the same purpose.

My zeal gave way to horror as I approached the station. The fitful lights picked out people huddled in shock and misery, bandaged heads and limbs, men hustling with difficulty up the embankment carrying a stretcher on which lay a motionless blanketed body. I fought the impulse to flee. Pushing my way toward the tracks, I was small enough to maneuver through the immense crowd that had gathered around the carnage.

It was the worst wreck to date in the history of the Long Island Rail Road, a head-on collision of two trains, one eastbound for Babylon, the other westbound for New York. The collision occurred on a short temporary stretch of single track set up to run trains in both directions while a construction project was under way. The engineer of the eastbound train had inexplicably failed to heed a stop signal and plowed straight into the oncoming train. Most of the casualties were from the front cars on both trains, which were split down the middle by the force of the collision. "It looked like a battlefield," one policeman said later.

"I never heard such screams. I'll hear them till I die."

More than forty doctors were at the scene, some still dressed in the tuxedos they had worn to a big event at the local hospital. It was hard to see at first through the haze of the blue light from the acetylene torches used to cut away the steel that was trapping bodies inside the cars. Scores of volunteer firemen aided the doctors in amputations performed by flashlight with only local anesthesia.

Ambulances arrived from as far away as twenty miles. In the glare of their floodlights, I saw at once that I wasn't needed. A half-dozen priests were moving through the wreckage, bending down to minister to those in pain, giving last rites, providing comfort to stricken relatives who had converged on the scene. This grotesque and terrifying scene was not the one I had rehearsed with my doll propped up on my pillow. My missionary theatrics completely vanished. My pretensions suddenly seemed ugly and absurd, and I longed for my orderly bedroom, for my glass cabinet of dolls and the set of Bobbsey Twins books beside my bed. I turned away and started home, running as fast as I could. Quietly, I let myself in through the front door, tiptoed carefully upstairs so as not to disturb the conversation of my parents and their guests in the dining room, put my coat under my bed, and fell into a troubled sleep.

The next morning, the collision was the talk of the village. Large headlines and photographs of the wreckage covered the front pages of the newspapers, along with a list of the twenty-nine people who had died. Obsessively, I tried to read each story. I repeated the names of the dead with grim curiosity: John Weeks, thirty, a graduate of Yale and an editor of *Time;* Harry Shedd 3d, a senior at Harvard who had temporarily suspended his studies to work at Simon & Schuster; Jefferson Allen, twenty-four, a glassblower killed along with his father, Charles; and Martin Steel, thirty-one, a veteran of nine campaigns in Italy and Germany during the Second World War. Their concise biographies seemed disconnected from the frightful scene that filled my mind. Images of mangled bodies pursued me, and every time I thought of that night, I squeezed back tears. Nor could I explain my inordinate fixation with the horrible night to my parents. Not only had I sneaked out of the house in the middle of the night, but I had made myself something they detested: a spectator to misery. My secret heaped yet another sin on my already endangered soul.

FEAR THAT another train crash could happen and that my father and all the men on our block might be found among the dead began to torment me. I begged my father to find another way to go to work. This was not possible, he explained. "Why don't you come with me tomorrow? We'll take the train together, spend the entire day at the Williams-

94

burg Bank, then take the train home. You'll see how safe it is." For as long as I could remember, I had awakened from sleep to the sound of my father showering and shaving in the bathroom across the hallway, preparing to leave for work. How often I had wished to accompany him into the city with all the other men instead of being left behind with the women and children. Now, if I could overcome my fear of the train, that wish could come true. "I'd love to," I said.

The next morning, my mother prepared bacon and eggs for my father and me. Though I was rarely hungry before school, on this morning I was determined to do whatever my father did. I ate my eggs over easy and sipped a cup of tea as he drank his coffee. While my father distributed his cigarettes, money clip, and watch into his jacket, pants, and vest pockets, my mother cleared the table, washed our cups and plates, and swept the floor. When she kissed us both goodbye, I felt a new sense of importance. Like soldiers off to war, we marched to the corner bus stop, falling in with the other men of our neighborhood. "Who is that young lady you're with this morning, Mike?" asked Mr. Rust with a pleasant smile. Across from the drugstore we boarded the bus, and moments later rolled past the streets that led to my grammar school, where all my less fortunate schoolmates would soon be assembling. In short order, the cross atop St. Agnes came into view and we pulled up to the Long Island Rail Road station.

When the train arrived, we headed directly for the last car, which was the smoking car. We found two seats together and my dad handed me the sports section of the *New York Daily News* to peruse while he lit a Chesterfield and leaned back to read the *Herald Tribune*. He seemed to know everyone in the car, and proudly introduced me to a half-dozen unfamiliar men. Across the aisle from us, a group of four men had turned their seats to face one another so they could play cards. Except for me, the entire car was filled with men. I paid little attention to their conversations about politics, their opinions of President Truman and the war in Korea, about which I knew little. When the talk turned to baseball, however, the confusion cleared and I became suddenly attentive.

The 1950 season was about to begin, and the Dodgers and the Red Sox were overwhelming favorites to win the championships of their leagues. But there were ominous signs: "I don't like this," muttered one man, shaking his head and glancing up from his newspaper. "Robinson's reported to camp twelve pounds overweight." Two fellow passengers shook their heads in agreement.

"Jackie Robinson will get himself in shape before the season starts," I interjected, as if I'd been personally attacked.

The men smiled indulgently.

Undeterred, I assured them, "You'll see on opening day."

"Newcombe's way off his rookie form, pitched

too much last year on two days' rest, the old sophomore jinx," another man chimed in.

"Don't worry," my father said, "Newk's slow spring probably doesn't mean anything."

Participation in their baseball conversation was so much fun I forgot my apprehension about the train ride, and we arrived in the city before I knew it, emerging at Atlantic Avenue in Brooklyn, right across from One Hansen Place, site of the Williamsburg Savings Bank building, which my father was then examining. The only Manhattan-style skyscraper in Brooklyn, the Williamsburg Savings Bank was built in 1929, around the same time as the Empire State and the Chrysler buildings. From its vast banking floor, designed to make every depositor feel like a millionaire, the building rose thirty-four stories to a tower adorned with the largest four-sided clock in the world. Capped by a golden dome, the Williamsburg Savings Bank was celebrated by Brooklyn residents as the "Tower of Strength." Over the years, my father had examined this bank so many times that he apparently felt an affiliation with the building itself. He gave an affectionate pat to one of the two lions, which guarded the main entrance, emblematic of the security offered by a savings bank. Metalwork silhouettes in the entrance gate represented the various crafts and occupations which had built and sustained the institution: electrician, carpenter, tile worker, machinist, plumber, ironworker.

The day's work was just beginning as we walked into the Main Banking Room, a cathedral of commerce, with its multicolored marble floor, stained-glass windows, and a ceiling of golden glass mosaic from which hung elaborate chandeliers. Customers were already beginning to line up at the teller windows as we took an elevator to the second-floor offices where my father and his fellow examiners worked. Beaming, I stood alongside him as he introduced me to about a dozen of his male colleagues and to several female secretaries.

After joining the banking department of New York State in his mid-twenties, my father had risen from bank examiner to senior examiner to principal examiner and eventually to supervising bank examiner, the highest level attainable for a civil-service employee. He was responsible for examining the top banks, such as Williamsburg, Morgan Guaranty Trust, Bank of New York. Examinations often took two or three months, with fifty or more examiners working under his supervision. In the 1940s and '50s, the exams involved a physical audit, a tallying of the cash on hand, and a field inspection of the collateral held on loans. There was a camaraderie between the examiners and the bank officials; often evaluations of the bank's loans would not begin until there was a bottle of rum or scotch on the table. On many occasions the examiners would talk informally with the bankers, telling them what steps they could take to prevent problems from arising. Despite this "old-boy club" atmosphere, my father never forgot that he was a public servant working for the people of New York and protecting their interests by making sure their banks were following sound practices.

"It's the greatest job in the world," he repeatedly told me. "I get to work with the best bunch of examiners. I never have a set routine...get to travel around the city every few months renewing old acquaintances, and at night no one's calling me saying, 'Kearns, get down here!' Why, you couldn't pay me to leave this job." At the time, it was commonplace for top examiners to be offered executive jobs with various banks, and on several occasions my father was offered the presidency or the vice-presidency of a bank he had examined. It would have brought him considerably more money, but when he claimed "you couldn't pay me to leave this job," he meant it.

My father found me my own desk with a comfortable leather chair. Completely satisfied, I tried to read the book I had brought along, *The Hidden Staircase,* while my dad went about his work, but I was happily distracted by the lively commotion all around me. My father took me to lunch in the executive dining room, with linen napkins and genuine silverware, and before the day ended, he led me into the giant vault. It took the clerk several minutes to spin the dial and open the enormous door, which was almost as thick as I was tall. Inside, my eye was drawn to hundreds of rectangular boxes where, my father explained, customers kept their most valuable possessions. We kept walking until we reached another door, which led to an interior vault; here I saw what seemed to me the riches of the world— bundles of ones, tens, fifties, and hundreds all neatly wrapped and piled in stacks that reached up almost as high as the ceiling itself.

We arrived home about six o'clock. My friends, as usual, were on the street playing, but the neighborhood seemed to have shrunk during my absence. Before this day, I had felt that my father and the other men had moved in a world of interests inaccessible to me; now I had glimpsed the other side, and I resolved someday to enter that larger world. I would go to work like my father, and yet I would somehow keep house the way my mother did, preparing lunch when the kids came home from school. How I would accomplish this I did not know, but the desire stayed with me.

Of more immediate importance, the trip to the bank with my dad brought my daily fears about the commuter train to an end. The images of the crushed bodies began to fade, and I no longer panicked when my father was ten minutes late returning from work. Whenever the gruesome memories flashed through my head, I simply substituted the images from my trip to the bank with my dad, replayed in my head the conversations I had had with the other men in the smoking car of the train. It worked. As ever, my father had understood the best way to calm my fears.

MY FIRST COMMUNION was scheduled for a Saturday morning at the end of May. As the big day approached, my preparations intensified. Over and over, my companions and I rehearsed proper behavior at Mass: how to make the sign of the cross, how to genuflect correctly, back held erect, right knee bent almost to the floor. We were drilled on when to sit and when to stand and when to kneel. For me, the hardest part, as ever, was keeping silent, the requirement that we not talk to our seatmates through the entire Mass.

The day before our First Communion, we were led into the church to make our First Confession. We had been told to examine our consciences and carefully consider the nature and number of our transgressions before reporting to the priest. For most of my friends there was little to worry about besides the usual fare for seven-year-olds: disobeying parents, talking in church, losing their temper. But I knew that, in addition to my sin of entering the Episcopal church, I had committed another sin, far from ordinary. For days, I plotted the best strategy for the necessary revelation. I would, I decided, immediately reveal my misdeed concerning the Episcopal church, and then camouflage the other sin amidst a host of smaller ones.

I opened the curtain and entered the confessional, a dark wooden booth built into the side wall of the church. As I knelt on the small worn bench, I could hear a boy's halting confession through the wall, his prescribed penance inaudible as the panel slid open on my side and the priest directed his attention to me.

"Yes, my child," he inquired softly.

"Bless me, Father, for I have sinned. This is my First Confession."

"Yes, my child, and what sins have you committed?"

"Well, Father, when Roy Campanella came to town three months ago, I wanted so badly to hear him speak that I went into the Episcopal church on the corner."

"And did you participate in a service that day?"

"Oh, no, Father, Roy's talk was in the parish hall, and there was no religious service at all."

"Well, then," he said, echoing what my father had told me at the time, "there is nothing here to worry about."

Oh, but there is, I thought, for I've only just begun my confession.

"And what else, my child?"

"I talked in church twenty times, I disobeyed my mother five times, I wished harm to others several times, I told a fib three times, I talked back to my teacher twice." I held my breath.

"And to whom did you wish harm?"

My scheme had failed. He had picked out the one group of sins that most troubled me. Speaking as softly as I could, I made my admission.

"I wished harm to Allie Reynolds."

"The Yankee pitcher?" he asked, surprise and concern in his voice. "And how did you wish to harm him?"

"I wanted him to break his arm."

"And how often did you make this wish?"

"Every night," I admitted, "before going to bed, in my prayers."

"And were there others?"

"Oh, yes," I admitted. "I wished that Robin Roberts of the Phillies would fall down the steps of his stoop, and that Richie Ashburn would break his hand."

"Is there anything else?"

"Yes, I wished that Enos Slaughter of the Cards would break his ankle, that Phil Rizzuto of the Yanks would fracture a rib, and that Alvin Dark of the Giants would hurt his knee." But, I hastened to add, "I wished that all these injuries would go away once the baseball season ended."

Encouraged by the priest's silence, I proceeded to describe sneaking out of the house the previous February and the more macabre thoughts that had arisen since the train wreck, when my sinful thoughts had expanded to encompass a desire that the train carrying the Yankees to Boston would fail to stop at a signal. My scenario left no permanent injuries but put the entire team out of action for the year, so that the Dodgers could finally win their first World Series.

"But how would you feel knowing that the victory wasn't really deserved," the priest asked, "knowing that if your rivals had been healthy your team might not have won? I promise you, it wouldn't feel anywhere near as good as if you won in the proper way. Now, let me tell you a secret. I love the Dodgers just as much as you do, but I believe they will win the World Series someday fairly and squarely. You don't need to wish harm on others to make it happen. Do you understand what I am saying?"

"Yes, Father."

"Are there any other sins, my child?"

"No, Father."

"For your penance, say two Hail Marys, three Our Fathers, and," he added, with a chuckle, "say a special prayer for the Dodgers. Now say the Act of Contrition."

"Oh, my God, I am heartily sorry for having offended Thee, and I detest all my sins...." When I finished, the priest made the sign of the cross and murmured the official Latin words of forgiveness. I left the confessional that day buoyant, my soul spotless. My First Confession, received by a baseball-loving priest, had left me closer to my church than ever before.

First Communion day broke with dazzling spring sunshine. My mother curled my hair, and I struggled into my new white dress with matching white anklets and shoes. My father took a roll of pictures before we left for the church, probably assuming that I wouldn't stay neat for long. One snapshot taken in our backyard caught my friend Eileen Rust and me standing together like two miniature brides, our hands clasped in prayer, looking straight at the camera with contented smiles. In another picture, I stand with my friend Lainie Lubar and her brother, Jeff. Though Lainie was Jewish, she, too, wore a white dress her mother had bought for her so that she might share in the celebration of our big day.

In the hallway of the school building next to the church, we were organized by height, girls in one line and boys, dressed in white jackets and white pants, in another. All together, there were about 150 children, desperately trying to remember everything we had been taught, concentrating on how to walk in perfect rows with our palms flat together and our fingers pointing upward to God. Led by two older girls dressed like angels, the procession left the school building and entered the church. I fervently wished that one day I could be chosen as an angel, but I knew that honor always fell to a St. Agnes girl rather than a girl from public school.

So intently did I fix my eyes on the floor tiles which served as our markers to hold a straight line that I almost tripped when I reached the proper pew. I settled in my seat and quickly turned my head to locate my parents, delighted to find them only ten rows back. Excitement mounted as the Mass proceeded, reaching a climax when the moment came to kneel before the priest, stick out my tongue, and receive the Host. I left the communion rail with the wafer in my mouth and stole a glance at my parents, who proudly smiled back. Fearing that the Host might fall out if I opened my mouth, however, I was afraid to return their smile. We had been told that we should swallow the Host whole, but my mouth was so dry from fasting—I had refrained even from water since the previous night—that it took me a long time to dislodge it from the roof of my mouth and maneuver it to a position where I could swallow. When I finally did swallow it, I was so relieved that I turned toward my parents, and stuck out my tongue to prove my task complete.

The nun at the end of my row cast me a withering look. I feared I had spoiled everything, for me and for my parents. But just at that moment, the most beautiful light—half red, half yellow—danced across the open page of my missal, and stayed with me as I turned the next page. It was simply the sun streaming through the stained-glass windows, but at that moment, I was certain that, despite my embarrassing lack of decorum, God had signaled His love on my First Communion day.

SINCE ONLY the truly blameless went directly to heaven, I knew I would have to spend some time in purgatory on the way. Given this inevitability, I was comforted by the doctrine of indulgences, which allowed me to reduce my sentence in the next world through suitable acts in this one. Almost every night I would recite three sets of prayers. The first set was to bolster my own spiritual position. The next set was for the poor souls already in purgatory who needed my help to move toward heaven. And the last was for my family and the Brooklyn Dodgers. At the end of each week I would add up the credits I had earned by the first set of prayers so that God might have an accurate record. "Dear God, I have said thirty Hail Marys, twenty Hail Holy Queens, forty Acts of Faith, and fifteen Acts of Hope, for a total of three hundred and fifty-five years off my life in purgatory. Please put this figure to my account. I live at One Twenty-five Southard Avenue, Rockville Centre, New York." I was less meticulous about calculating the worth of the second set of prayers. Souls in purgatory probably kept better track of these things, I decided, having little else to do.

The mysteries of Catholicism contained less mundane and quantitative means to salvation. We were taught that if, at a certain point in the Mass, you looked at the cross with absolute reverence in your heart, you would receive a full remission of all the sins you had committed. At the appropriate moment, I would hold my breath, and stare unmovingly at the crucified Jesus with all the reverence I could summon. Unfortunately, it was impossible to know if your reverence was adequately intense. So nightly prayers remained necessary, at least for peace of mind. On more than one occasion, however, I awoke with a start, still kneeling by my bed, having fallen asleep in the middle of my lengthy attempt to cover all the bases.

Chief among my prayers for the Dodgers was my wish that they win the World Series before too many years passed by. "Please, God, let this year be the year. My father has been following the Dodgers since he was a little boy and he's never seen them win the Series. I would like that for him. And I would like it for me, because it would feel so great to wake up in the morning after the victory and know that the Dodgers were the best team in the world. Thank you, God."

These prayers became more urgent as the 1950 season got under way with a crushing 9–1 loss to the Phillies. By the All-Star break, the Dodgers were in fourth place, behind the Phillies, Cards, and Braves. Pitching was the problem. Rex Barney, as usual, was having trouble getting the ball over the plate, Ralph Branca was tiring after four or five innings, Dan Bankhead had an ailing arm, and Don Newcombe was unable to pitch the way he had his spectacular rookie year. Only Preacher Roe kept the Dodgers in contention.

In August, though improved pitching and hot bats had moved us into second place, there seemed little chance of catching the Phillies. Nevertheless, there were fabulous moments. At the end of the month, I sat with my dad listening to my favorite kind of game, a 19–3 blowout of the Braves. No anxiety, no need to duck out and walk around the block when the opposing team was at bat, just pleasure that deepened as the even-tempered first baseman Gil Hodges hit one, then two, then three home runs. By the time he stepped up to the plate in the eighth, everyone was rooting for Hodges to make history by hitting four home runs in a single game. Since 1900, Red Barber told us, only three men had hit four home runs in one game, and two of them had needed extra innings to accomplish their feat. Only the immortal Lou Gehrig had hit four in regulation innings. We could hear the fans chanting as Hodges worked the count to two and two and then let go with a monstrous swing that sent the ball into the upper seats of the left-field stands. The roar of the crowd couldn't have been louder if the Dodgers had clinched the pennant.

Elation at Hodges' accomplishment was short-lived, however, as the Dodgers slipped into third, falling behind the Braves as well as the Phillies. On September 18, they were nine games behind Philadelphia with only seventeen left to play. Nothing but a miracle could save the season, people said. And it did indeed seem that divine inspiration descended upon the Dodgers in those last weeks of September, when they launched a remarkable winning streak that coincided with a collapse of both the Phillies and the Braves. Their amazing run brought Brooklyn within two games of first with two left to play. And the last two games were against the first-place Phillies!

After the Dodgers won the first game, 7–3, they needed only one more win to have come further faster than any team in history, forcing a playoff starting in Brooklyn the following day. The final game, a duel between Don Newcombe and Robin Roberts, was so tense that I could barely listen. The two teams were locked in a 1–1 tie when the Dodgers came to bat in the bottom of the ninth. Cal Abrams, a young outfielder who lived in Levittown, not far from Rockville Centre, drew a lead-off walk and reached second when Pee Wee Reese singled to left. With no outs and Abrams in scoring position, I began to relax a little, certain that one of the next three batters—Snider, Robinson, or Furillo—would somehow push over the winning run.

Now, if Snider would bunt Abrams to third, a fly ball could bring him in. But Dodger manager Burt Shotton had Snider hit away, a surprise move that seemed to work perfectly when Snider singled to center. As Abrams rounded third heading toward home, I was certain we had won the game and forced the Phillies into a playoff. Then, suddenly, everything unraveled. Expecting Snider to bunt, Richie Ashburn had positioned himself in shallow center field. Not needing to charge the ball, he fielded it quickly and threw a perfect strike to home plate that allowed Phillies catcher Stan Lopata to tag Abrams out.

Once again, as in 1941, when Owens dropped the third strike, Dodger fans were left with the indelible image of defeat being snatched from the jaws of victory.

At least Reese and Snider had advanced to third and second with the throw home, so a fly ball could still win the game. But after Robinson was intentionally walked to load the bases, Furillo popped out and Hodges hit a fly to right for the final out. I knew with a grim certainty that when the Phillies came to bat in the top of the tenth it was over for my Dodgers, even though we'd have another chance at the bottom of the inning. The first two Phillies singled, and then Dick Sisler hit a long home run to left, giving the Whiz Kids a 4–1 victory and their first pennant in thirty-five years.

When the World Series started between the Phillies and the Yankees, I hardly cared who won. I despised both Allie Reynolds and Robin Roberts, and when they faced off against one another, the less I heard the better. Elaine was terribly annoying when the Yankees swept the powerful Whiz Kids, but not so insufferable as she would have seemed had my Dodgers been the victims.

AT THE CONCLUSION of the baseball season in early autumn, I turned my full attention to school. Every morning, Elaine and I walked to the Morris School, our notebooks and pencil cases in hand. At noon, the entire grammar school was dismissed for an hour and fifteen minutes so we could walk home for lunch and return for the afternoon session. It was a pleasant walk, especially on crisp autumn days when the fallen leaves, raked up in curbside heaps to be burned on weekends by our fathers, crunched beneath our shoes. Along the way, we filled our pencil cases with acorns, ammunition for our fights with the boys. The distance from Southard Avenue being about three-quarters of a mile, we walked three miles a day.

The Morris Grammar School was a faded red brick two-story building flanked on one side by a large playing field with a baseball diamond and basketball court for the boys, and on the other by a narrower playground with slides and swings for the girls. When the first bell called us from the playground, we hung up our coats in the cloakroom and sat at our desks. The top of the desks lifted up to form a drawer in which we kept our pencil cases, books, and the countless notes we passed to one another throughout our classes. A second bell officially began the day, signaling us to rise and pledge our allegiance to the flag of the United States, which stood in the corner. Having paid homage to country, we bowed our heads to ask God's blessing, repeating aloud the Lord's Prayer. Some of my Jewish friends joined in the prayer; others remained silent, heads bowed. Since the Catholic amens followed abruptly upon "and deliver us from evil," and the Protestants continued on—

"For thine is the kingdom and the power and the glory..."—you could distinguish Catholic from Protestant by noting where the amens fell.

We stayed in the same classroom all day, learning math and reading and practicing the Palmer method of penmanship on lined sheets of paper that resembled music staffs. One of my teachers had devised an elaborate system for rewarding achievement. For each book read or report completed, we were awarded a blue star on the blackboard. Ten blue stars equaled a red star, and five red stars earned a gold star. We eagerly awaited the posting of the stars at the day's end, hoping each time that we had earned the coveted gold star. For me, that day never arrived. Although I probably accumulated more stars for books read than anyone else in my class, stars could be subtracted if we disobeyed an order or talked in class. Since I rarely stopped talking, I lost stars almost as quickly as I earned them through the day. I watched in dismay as my red stars were erased and my blue stars halved. The injustice of rescinding a reward for a book completed or report written and judged acceptable deeply rankled me. My only solution, however, was to stop talking in class, and this, even for the glory of the gold star, I was unable to do.

We constructed shoe-box dioramas of the Pilgrims and the Indians, did reports on the revolution and the Civil War, and completed projects on the settlement of the West. We read about the Statue of Liberty, Ellis Island, and the waves of immigrants that had come to America from all over the world. Everyone in our class had to give a report on where his or her ancestors had lived. Our teacher placed a little flag of each country of origin on a world map in the front of the room. Almost every part of Western Europe, Central Europe, and Russia was represented by a flag. There were, however, no flags from Latin America or Asia. Not yet. The teacher stressed that America was a special country, because, despite the diversity of our racial, religious, and ethnic origins, we were all one nation, one people with a shared set of values and a common culture. Our textbooks gave us a unifying vision of individuals from all different nations, melting into a new, distinctly American race. Only later would we come to understand that the melting pot did not melt everybody, that racism deprived men and women of color of the equal opportunity promised in the American creed. Only later, as historian Arthur Schlesinger has observed, would we "imagine the arrival of Columbus from the viewpoint of those who met him as well as those who sent him."

Both my parents showered me with praise for the smallest achievements and spent hours going over my homework, preparing me for tests, and helping me with projects. Just as my mother had helped me learn my catechism, she drilled me in the state capitals, the amendments to the Constitution, the names of the explorers, the dates of the Missouri Compromise, the Dred Scott Decision, the sinking of the U.S.S. *Maine*. When I had to prepare a report on Mexico, my father brought home an entire briefcase filled with books, maps, and brochures. The more you read about a subject, he advised me, the more interesting it will seem.

The Rockville Centre Public Library became one of my favorite buildings in town. When my mother wasn't feeling well, she would send me to the library with titles of books she wanted to read. Since I now had a card of my own, I took great pride in checking out her books as well as mine. In those days, each book had a sheet glued to the last page on which the librarian stamped the due date and cardholder's number. It was possible to count how many others had read the same book. I liked the thought that the book I was now holding had been held by dozens of others; it made me sad for both the author and the book when I discovered that I was the only one to take a particular volume off a shelf for months or even years.

As long as I could remember, my mother and I talked about books. In the early days, she would ask me to summarize in my own words the book she had read aloud. Now she would often get me to sit by her side and read to her. With all the dramatic effect I could muster, I picked out chapters of the book I was reading at the moment. I blithely assumed she would find my children's books as absorbing as I did. I especially liked books that were written in series. As I opened each new volume of Nancy Drew, there was her blue roadster, her father, Carson Drew, and her kindly housekeeper, Hannah Gruen. These details provided a sense of comfort and contributed to a feeling of mastery as I progressed through the series. When I discovered an author I liked, I wanted to read everything he or she had written. Weeks spent with Louisa May Alcott were followed by months with Robert Louis Stevenson. From my mother's reading of *The Jungle Book* and the *Just So Stories*, I turned to *Captains Courageous* and *Kim*.

WHEN I WAS in the third grade, I was assigned an oral report on Franklin Roosevelt, who I knew had been president when I was born. After I had insisted on talking about Roosevelt every night for a week, my parents decided to take me to Hyde Park to visit the house in which young Franklin had grown up, and which had anchored his entire life. On a chaise longue in Roosevelt's bedroom I saw Fala's leash resting on the plaid blanket where the little dog had slept. And sitting on a small desk in the study were the president's cigarette holder and his pince-nez glasses, exactly where he had left them at the end of the day. The house was called a museum, but it seemed to me a home where people lived. And I was sure it was only a matter of time before Roosevelt would return, pick up his cigarette holder, put on his glasses, and sit down to read, patting his dog at his side. I realized that day I could play an inner game with history just as I did with baseball. If I closed my eyes I could visualize Roosevelt in his room with Fala, just as, when I listened to the stories my father told, I could see the great players of the past—Babe Ruth and Lou Gehrig and Zack Wheat—knock the mud from their cleats, settle into the batter's box, narrow their eyes on the pitcher, and unleash their majestic swings.

CHAPTER FOUR

A black delivery van pulled up to the front entrance of the house next door. My parents and I watched from the window as a uniformed driver dismounted, opened the gate of the van, and wheeled a large wooden crate toward the visibly excited assemblage of the Goldschmidt family standing at the front door.

Television had come to the neighborhood.

That night, the parents and children of Southard Avenue crowded into the Goldschmidts' living room, and watched as vaguely defined, snowy figures cavorted across the seven-inch black-and-white screen embedded in an odd block of furniture. "A marvel," the adults assured one another, as Mr. Goldschmidt continually adjusted the metal rod of the antenna. But to me and my playmates, it was only another wonder in a world of constantly unfolding wonders, like the stories my mother told me, the first book I read, or my first trip to Ebbets Field.

When the Goldschmidts bought their television in 1946, there were only seven thousand sets in use in the entire country, and theirs was the only one on our block. Within months, the number doubled when the Lubars' living room became the home of a nine-inch set with a slightly better picture, which became an irresistible attraction for all the children on the block. Almost every afternoon we would congregate on the Lubars' front stoop, waiting expectantly, and often vocally, for the invitation to enter, so we could sit cross-legged on the floor and watch the amazing parade of puppets, comedians, and cowboys which marched across their tiny screen.

It was only a matter of time, spurred by embarrassment at our imposition on the Lubars, before every family on our block had a set. And the pattern in our neighborhood, where desire begot what seemed like necessity, was repeated across America. By 1950, there were sets in three million homes; from then on, sales grew at a rate of five million a year, until, by the end of the decade, more than fifty million families would own a television.

When our own ten-inch table console finally arrived, my parents invited everyone on the block to come over for a Sunday-afternoon showing of *The Super Circus*. That morning, my mother set out hot dog rolls and hamburger buns, prepared a salad, put extra chairs in the living room for the grown-ups, and laid a blanket on the floor for the children. The entrance of the handsome ringmaster into the center ring, dressed in a sequined costume, was greeted by a low, admiring whistle from Elaine's grandmother, and the circus began. We giggled at the antics of the clowns, marveled at the sight of the stately lions, and gasped at the daring of the high-wire artists.

To me, the afternoon was more memorable and exciting than my trip to see the actual Ringling Brothers Circus in Madison Square Garden. But not because of television. As a result of my mother's illness, I almost never had a group of friends at my home, to say nothing of the entire neighborhood. On this Sunday, however, I was a hostess, bringing someone a second hot dog, refilling the bowl of potato chips, constantly looking around to see what needs I could fill. Even though everyone was looking at the television set, I felt as if I were on stage, playing a role I thoroughly enjoyed. As soon as the show was over, and the guests departed, I asked my mother if we could do this every week, making our house the center of Sunday activity. "I'm sorry," my mother said, "but I simply can't do it. Even now, I am so exhausted just from having everyone here that I've got to lie down for a little while. But I'll tell you what, if you'd like to pick one show each week and have all the kids over to see it, I think that would be fine."

I picked *Howdy Doody*, my favorite show, featuring a freckled puppet in a plaid shirt, dungarees, and cowboy boots; an affable ventriloquist, Buffalo Bob, in fringed buckskin; and a "Peanut Gallery," composed of the luckiest kids in the world. At 5:25 P.M., we gathered before the set, staring at NBC's test pattern for five minutes before Buffalo Bob's booming voice opened the show: "Say, kids, what time is it?" "It's Howdy Doody Time," we shrieked in reply. The pitch of excitement continued as Clarabell the clown sneaked up behind Buffalo Bob to shoot water in his face, and we laughed so hard our stomachs hurt. Only when Buffalo Bob said good night and the kids in the Peanut Gallery waved goodbye did we finally calm down, and my friends disperse for dinner.

When the Friedles bought their thirteen-inch console, we flocked to their house on Tuesday evenings to watch Milton Berle; the Lubars' house became our scheduled stop for the Saturday-morning cartoons. We gathered to watch TV's first interplanetary heroes: Tom Corbett, Captain Video, and Superman. I was visiting Eileen Rust when their television set arrived. The box was unimpressive, and Eileen began to cry, fearing that her set would have the smallest screen in the neighborhood. We watched as the carton was opened to reveal a giant eighteen-inch set, the largest on the block. Eileen gasped and the rest of us began to clap. Suddenly, Eileen's house became the most desirable place to gather.

Television entered our lives robed as the

bearer of communal bonds, providing a new set of common experiences, block parties, and festive gatherings shared by children and adults alike. The fantasies of television slowly infiltrated our own. After the first soap operas, *Search for Tomorrow* and *Love of Life,* appeared on the air in the fall of 1951, our mothers could be found in spirited conversation discussing the behavior of their favorite characters and debating the likely outcome of their latest difficulties as if they were another family on the block. For days, our parents discussed the dramatic reaction of Elaine's seventyfive-year-old great-grandmother, Amelia, to the kidnapping of the little girl, Patti, on *Search for Tomorrow.* Patti was the six-year-old daughter of Joanne Barron, a young widow whose rich in-laws had kidnapped the child after losing a custody battle. A desperate week-long chase ended as police helped Joanne pursue the child's kidnappers through woods, which, in the early days of live television, consisted simply of a dark area filled with a maze of music stands affixed with branches to represent trees. Finding Patti's shoes near a pond, the searchers feared she had drowned, though viewers knew she was still alive in the hands of her evil grandmother.

At this point in the drama, Amelia, her print housedress flapping, her white hair disheveled, came rushing into the street, alarm in her voice. She demanded that we call the police and tell them where Patti was. By doing nothing, she insisted, we were endangering the life of this lovely child. Futilely, our mothers tried to explain that the show was a fictional drama, that Joanne and her daughter were actresses following a script. But Amelia refused to believe it, and we could do nothing to assuage her anxiety until the next episode, when Patti was found and returned to her mother.

The confusion of television with reality was not limited to the very old. One evening, my television screen revealed Joan of Arc being burned at the stake. There, before my eyes, the young woman stood, lashed to a piling atop a pyre in the old marketplace in Rouen, France. A male voice denounced her as a heretic who must pay for her sins with her life. She was, he said, like a rotten branch that must be severed to preserve the tree. "It is not true," Joan cried. "I am a good Christian." Her words went unheeded. The fire crackled and the flames consumed her. Stunned by this violence taking place in front of me, I raced into the kitchen to find my mother. She reassured me that no one was being hurt, that the program was simply one of a series of historical dramatizations, called *You Are There*, narrated by Walter Cronkite. Through re-enactments and "eyewitness" accounts, the series endeavored to provide viewers with a sense that they were actually present at important moments in history. My anxiety was replaced by embarrassment at my naïveté, and I returned to the screen. In the weeks that followed, I watched the capture of John Wilkes Booth, the siege of the Alamo, the fall of Fort Sumter, the signing of the Declaration of Independence, the surrender of Robert E. Lee at Appomattox, and the duel between Hamilton and Burr.

For me, however, the flow of drama and entertainment was of small consequence beside the glorious opportunity to watch my Dodgers on the screen. In 1951, for the first time, I could follow the Dodgers for a full season on television. I watched Gil Hodges stretch to snag a skidding grounder and throw to the pitcher covering first; saw Carl Furillo as he barehanded a ball that bounced off the right-field wall and then fired to second to catch a runner trying to extend a single into a double; and glimpsed the smile flicker across Robinson's face as he crossed home plate with the winning run.

THE BASEBALL SEASON of 1951 would be seared into the memory of every Dodger fan, its scar carried across the years as the progress of lives took old New Yorkers to different parts of the country. Not long ago, I was talking about the last game of the '51 season with friends in the lounge of a San Francisco hotel. A man seated at the adjoining table— tall, distinguished, a prosperous executive from the miracle factories of Silicon Valley— leaned over, a mournful tone in his voice. "I remember," he said. "I was there." I knew immediately what he meant.

The rivalry between the Dodgers and the Giants was unlike any other in baseball. Even in years when the two teams were not contending for the pennant, every meeting was regarded as a separate war, to be fought with implacable hostility. For twenty or thirty hours before the first pitch, thousands of fans would line up in front of Ebbets Field or the Polo Grounds in hopes of buying a ticket before the game sold out. After the last inning, the arguments overflowed to the streets and bars of Brooklyn and New York. But in 1951, this historic rivalry entered a new dimension, reached a level of intensity never before attained and never to be surpassed.

Over family dinners, and in our daily encounters, children and parents alike discussed and analyzed the reports from spring training which carried the first hints that this would be no ordinary season. Although every manager is publicly optimistic before a season starts, the braggadocio of Giant manager Leo Durocher was both irritating and ominous, heightened by my father's belief that Durocher was a great manager. Durocher had managed the Dodgers for six years in the forties, when he was beloved in Brooklyn and despised in New York. Then, in one of the more grotesque twists of baseball history, he left the Dodgers to manage the Giants, becoming their champion and our nemesis.

During spring training, Durocher, now known to us as "Leo the Lip," proclaimed that the '51 Giants would have the best pitching in the National League, with Sal Maglie, Larry Jansen, Jim Hearn, and Dave Koslo. To me, even the thought of the scowling, bearded Maglie was a kind of nightmare, his face the one I would most dread if it appeared in my window. He was called "the Barber," because, when he saw fit, his high, tight fastballs nearly shaved hitters' chins. To make things worse, Giant slugger Bobby Thomson was ripping the ball in spring training with the authority he had shown in 1949, when he had driven in over one hundred runs and paced the Giants' attack. "We have the pitching, the power, and the speed," Durocher said; "what else can any manager ask?"

The Dodgers, by contrast, had floundered all spring: Newcombe and Campanella were overweight; Hodges began camp late because his wife had given birth to their second baby. The team seemed to lack focus. Its play was shoddy. I agonized over the box score of every defeat as if it were the World Series. My father tried to explain that Dodger manager Chuck Dressen was more concerned with evaluating players and selecting a lineup than with winning preseason ball games. "Except for the pitching," he explained, "we've got the best team in the National League, hands down. Just say the names." He smiled. "Campanella, Hodges, Robinson, Reese; Snider, the best center fielder in either league right now; Furillo, the best arm in baseball. Just say the names, honey, and relax."

But I couldn't stop worrying, my own anxiety fed by the smiling, confident boasts of my friends and rivals in the butcher shop. "It's going to be our year, Ragmop," they told me, while choosing a cut of meat for my mother. "But don't worry, your time will come." To me at the age of eight, however, no appeal to the future could possibly compensate for the prospect of failure in the present. *This* was my time.

Durocher's widely circulated claim that he had the "best pitching staff in baseball," along with my father's insistence that pitching was our only weakness, forced me to shift my attention away from Robinson, Snider, and Campanella, our titans of hitting, to the bizarre figure of Dodger pitcher Rex Barney, whose problems with control threatened to end his once-promising career. When Barney had first come up in 1943, he'd been compared with Bob Feller and Walter Johnson. With the best fastball in the league, he had pitched a no-hitter against the Giants and had struck out Joe DiMaggio with bases loaded in the World Series. But on the final day of the '48 season, he broke his leg sliding into second base, and ever after he seemed to have lost both his rhythm and his control. Even after a good start, if he threw a few bad pitches in a row, he would suddenly fall apart, unable to find the plate, throwing well above and behind the batter into the screen, bouncing the ball into the dirt, hitting three or four batters in a row. Branch Rickey had taken Barney to a psychiatrist, put him on a special diet, and made him memorize pages of Charles Dickens every night to improve his concentration. Nothing worked. Barney became so desperate, he later admitted, that he contemplated jumping off buildings and bridges.

Now, Dressen announced, under the new regime, Barney would be treated like any other pitcher, rather than like a freak. No more psychiatrists, no more Dickens, no more pitching between two clotheslines for two extra hours every day. With this new approach, Dressen believed, Barney would recover the form that had promised to place him among the premier pitchers in baseball and strengthen our problematic rotation of Newcombe, Erskine, Roe, and Branca. But we all knew that this year was Rex Barney's last chance.

THAT SPRING, fortunately, my attention was diverted from baseball by a sporting tradition of our own. My sister Jeanne was selected co-captain of the Blue Team at her high school. As it had for more than three decades, the South Side Senior High School had divided all the girls into a Red Team and a Blue Team for an Olympic-style competition. Each team would begin with an elaborate opening presentation, a pageant of marches, songs, and dances all organized around a unifying theme. After the judges had scored the opening ceremony, the athletic events began: basketball, stunts-and-tumbling, volleyball, relay races. The victor in each event (including a poster contest and a cheerleading display) would receive a specified number of points. On the final night of competition, following an often spectacular finale in which all four hundred girls participated, the points were tallied and a winner was proclaimed.

At a time when there were no opportunities for girls to play in Little League or participate in varsity-level sports, the Red and Blue Meet attracted the attention of the entire town. For six weeks, the high-school girls, divided between two teams, thought of little else. They practiced for hours after school each day, and spent every weekend at school. Our house was at the center. My sister's selection had transformed our quiet rooms into a frenzied arena, crowded with girls sewing costumes, writing songs, and practicing their dance steps. I would rush home from school, and in a state of almost perpetual excitement, I hovered at the edge of activity. I felt no one could possibly surpass the Blue Team's brilliant theme. All of their routines would constitute a "Museum of Headlines," each dance performance emblematic of an important event in American history, such as the revolution, the Emancipation Proclamation, or the achievement of women's suffrage.

My mother seemed unbothered by the unprecedented confusion as she helped with the costumes and happily stirred a big vat of blue dye into which five hundred clothespins were dipped to create the team emblems. Our house seemed to have become a different place. Needless to say, this was a special occasion for Jeanne, and my mother made the most concentrated effort to open up our house and make it a place where Jeanne could exercise her role as co-captain. Loyalty to Jeanne's team prevented me from wearing any color but blue for six weeks straight: blue underpants, blue socks, and blue shoelaces as well as blue skirts and blouses.

The night before the competition, the school held a Mother and Daughter Banquet, which served as a dress rehearsal for the songs and cheers. I wandered into my parents' room as my mother dressed, watching as she stood in her bra and panties and pulled her armor-like girdle over her thin hips. She wriggled her nylons up her long legs, fastened them to the rubbery flaps that hung down from her girdle, put on a full slip to smooth the ridges of the girdle, and finally dropped a lovely blue silk dress over her head and shoulders. She let me pick out her earrings and help fasten a silver bracelet on her wrist. With high blue pumps, and a spritz of perfume on her neck, she was ready to go. When my father came home that night, he whistled at her graceful pirouette in the middle of the living-room floor.

After my mother and sister left, my dad took me to dinner at Shor's, my favorite place for hamburgers, and then to Jahn's, an old-fashioned ice-cream parlor. For a while, we talked about Rex Barney, who, in his most recent outing, had thrown thirty-one straight balls, walked seven, hit one batter, thrown one wild pitch, and almost decapitated three batters before mercifully being pulled—and all in two-thirds of an inning! Dressen's laissez-faire regime was producing no better results than Rickey's old methods. The club was beginning to concede that Barney was a lost cause. Suddenly, my father interrupted my running commentary on the ill-fated Barney, turned to me, and said: "That dress was just the right color for your mother." I was struck by the light in his eye and the tone of his voice as he continued, "Didn't you think she looked lovely tonight?"

There was standing room only the next evening when the town converged on the high-school gym to watch the three-hour meet. I cheered every performance by the Blue Team, and struggled to remain silent when the Red Team came on stage. When Jeanne's team was proclaimed the winner by a narrow margin, I leaped from my seat for a final yell, only to find I was so hoarse from screaming I could no longer speak. So I watched in compelled silence as Jeanne and the captain were lifted up in the air by their exultant teammates and, for the first time, I became aware that the camaraderie and pride of competition involved in sports was not limited to the world of men.

As the Giants prepared to return north, their impressive performance in spring training had brought euphoria to the meat market. "Hey, Ragmop," the butchers preened as I stopped by the shop on my way home from school. "Did you hear that Jim Hearn pitched a three-hitter today? And how about those back-to-back homers from Monte Irvin and Bobby Thomson?"

"Don't talk to me about Irvin and Thomson," I countered somewhat defensively. "Snider and Hodges will hit twice as many homers. Did you see how they crushed the ball yesterday?"

"Yeah," Max said, smiling, "but we're winning and you're not."

Stung by the truth of this comment, I fell back on my father's mantra. "Just wait till opening day, when it counts; then we'll see who's better."

Shortly before opening day, Joe and Max beckoned me in as I walked past the market. Since this would certainly be a glorious season, they explained, they had decided to make a special window display of the relative fortunes of the Giants and the Dodgers. (Presumably no other team really counted.) On a big bulletin board they would fill in the daily total of runs, hits, and errors for the Giants, and, they informed me, I had been specially selected to do the same for the Dodgers. Thus the entire neighborhood would know exactly how each team was doing on a daily basis. I accepted with delight, imagining myself well on the way to becoming the Red Smith of Rockville Centre, the scribe upon whom which all my neighbors would depend.

"Don't take the first game too seriously," my father reassured me after an opening-day loss to the Phillies, but I remembered the previous season, when we had lost the pennant by a single game. It was conceivable that this single loss could once again spell victory or defeat. After opening day, however, the Dodgers began to soar. By the end of April, they were in first place, while the Giants, after losing eleven games in a row, had tumbled into the cellar. "It's like a snake eating its young," Durocher explained. "The thing starts, the guys start to press, the worse it gets." As I went into the butcher shop each day to post my totals, I didn't want to gloat, although concealing my happiness was beyond my powers. "Don't worry," I said, somewhat condescendingly, and quite pleased with my own generosity of spirit, "there are still lots of games left. The season is young. Anything can happen."

DURING THE AFTERNOON of the last day of April, all over the neighborhood, children waited restlessly for their fathers to return from work. We were all going to Ebbets Field for "Rockville Centre Night," an annual tradition established several years earlier to celebrate the fact that a member of the Brooklyn team, outfielder Dixie Walker, known as "the People's Cherce," had chosen to make his home among us.

My father and I boarded one of the dozen buses which would transport more than seven hundred residents of Rockville Centre to

Brooklyn. No sooner had we arrived at the park than, with my father's permission, I ran toward the crowd of kids already lining the rail behind the Dodger dugout. Like a pantheon of gods, they were all there, Jackie and Duke, Campy and Gil, just a few feet away, talking to the kids who were waiting in line for autographs. But by the time I got there the lines were already too long, and even though I joined the group attending on Jackie Robinson, I knew I was too far back to reach him before the game started. Dismayed, I looked along the dugout and saw rookie pitcher Clem Labine standing alone and unattended toward the end of the rail. Only the week before, Jimmy Cannon had written that the Dodgers had great expectations for the tall right-hander. More important to me than his prospects, however, was the fact that he probably represented my only chance to get an autograph. Breaking away from the Robinson line, pen in hand, I rushed over to Labine, and was rewarded with a pleased smile and a signature. Grasping my prize, I moved back along the rail. But, still unable to get close to the other players, I soon returned to the available Labine.

"Weren't you just here?" he asked with a grin.

"Oh, yes," I explained, scrambling for an explanation, "but if I have two of your autographs, I can keep one and trade the other for a Jackie Robinson."

"No kidding," he said, his eyes widening, "you could trade me even up for Robinson?

Well, that's something," he said, shaking his head, and I thought I detected a bounce to his step when he strode back toward the field, where our high-school band was beginning to assume formation for the pregame exhibition.

On earlier trips to Ebbets Field, I had felt part of the invisible community of Dodger fans, linked by shared emotions and experience to thousands of strangers who, for a few hours, were not strangers at all. But tonight was different. All around me, in the sections of the grandstand set aside for our town, were the familiar figures of my mundane daily life. It was as if my block, my school, my church had been snatched up and transported to a gigantic ocean liner for a trip to some fantastic land. I recognized all the people, of course, but they were not the same. The familiar setting of our lives, the context we shared, had changed and, in changing, had imparted a different dimension to my existence. The invisible barriers dividing the natural compartments of my life had been dissolved, leaving me a resident of a larger world.

Out on the field, I could see George Wilson, the high-school bandleader, who had recently moved to our block with his wife and two girls. After school, Mr. Wilson gave music lessons in his home, the wail of saxophones and trombones spilling out into our spring afternoons. Now, resplendent in a bright-red uniform with brass buttons and gold epaulets, he stood with solemn dignity in front of his forty-five-member band, waiting while Red Barber himself introduced the mayor of Rockville Centre. After a few welcoming remarks, we rose and Mr. Wilson signaled the band to begin an impressive rendition of "The Star-Spangled Banner."

A few seats to my right, I saw Doc Schimmenti, wearing a blue Dodger shirt instead of the white pharmacist's jacket which had always seemed as much a part of his appearance as his kindly face or his slicked-back hair. I almost didn't recognize my teacher, Miss Levitt, until she said hello to me. Standing before our class, she had always been primly dressed, her hair pulled back in a tight bun. Here, seated in the next row, she was wearing pedal pushers, her legs exposed, her hair hanging loosely over her shoulders. And I had to conceal my laugh as I looked over and could swear I saw—cracking roasted peanuts and brushing the shells from her habit—my First Communion teacher, Sister Marian, from St. Agnes. Mr. Rust sat behind us with his son, Eddie, not far from Mr. Greene, who had brought his two sons, Kent and Jay. Twenty or thirty feet over to my right, Max and Joe from the butcher shop waved sheepishly to me, somewhat subdued since everyone knew they were rabid Giant fans. At the top of our section, Miss Newton, our grammar-school principal, held a sign on which twelve big teardrops had been painted to suggest the grief of the Giants as they faced the prospect of losing their twelfth game in a row.

But the tears were not to flow. The Giants

took a large lead in the early innings. In the bottom of the third, the loudspeaker announced that rookie Clem Labine was entering the game in relief. For luck, I pressed my two autographs in my hand and watched with proprietary pleasure as he cooled off the Giants with two hitless innings. But for me the real drama of the game was the confrontation between the player I liked best, Jackie Robinson, and the player I detested and feared, Sal Maglie. In the first inning, we cheered when Robinson got up from the ground after a Maglie bean ball and hit a home run. Robinson was still angry when he came to bat in the fourth. The first pitch was right at his head. I covered my eyes with my hands, wanting to look away, fearing that something bad was going to happen. For weeks reporters had been warning that a dangerous bean-ball feud was under way between the Dodgers and the Giants. There had been ugly incidents in each of the five games they had played. In their very first encounter, Dodger pitcher Chris Van Cuyk had forced Henry Thompson to the ground with a pitch that exploded dangerously close to his head. In the next game, Carl Furillo, whose skull had been fractured by a Giant pitcher two years earlier, had been driven into the dirt. In the game after that, Robinson was hit by a pitch that left a bad swelling and a deep discoloration of his arm.

I peeked through my fingers to see Robinson drag a bunt down the first-base line. Maglie ran to cover first. Although the ball rolled foul, Robinson barreled into Maglie so hard the pitcher was thrown to the ground. Players from both teams spilled out onto the field, and Robinson's teammates had to pull him away from Maglie. A loud chorus of boos followed Robinson as he walked back to the plate. Never before had I heard Robinson booed at Ebbets Field. From behind me, someone yelled, "That's a dirty trick, Jackie. Who do you think you are?"

"Who do you think *you* are?" I shouted back and was appalled to confront none other than Mr. Rust. He looked as surprised as I felt, but before either of us could speak, the angry roar burst into cheers as Robinson singled to left. When the Dodgers scored a few more times, it seemed they might climb back into the game, but time ran out, and the Giants won by a score of 8–5.

The next day, Robinson explained that he had deliberately created the disturbance to force league action on the bean-ball feud before someone really got hurt. "I don't believe people come to ballparks to fight or see fights, but this business of maliciously throwing at batters' heads has got to be stopped," he was reported saying. "The rule book specifically says the umpires must take action on bean balls. Not one of them has moved. I don't care if I'm fined, but I'm telling you I bunted and ran into Maglie deliberately to bring this whole thing to a head....This has got to stop. I hope what I did helps stop it. I don't want to have to do it again but if I have to I will."

But it didn't stop. Durocher answered Robinson by saying that what made Maglie such a great pitcher was his willingness to throw at a batter when the situation demanded it. When Maglie was out there, Durocher said, it was him or the hitter. "I'll throw at anybody," Maglie added. "That's part of the game. I've got to do it to protect myself against hitters leaning in on my curve." So the feud continued, making each successive Dodger-Giant game that season more flammable and nerve-racking than the last. It almost seemed as if the season was moving toward some kind of tragic ending. And it was, but not one I had ever imagined.

ALTHOUGH THE GIANTS improved steadily through the month of May, the Dodgers remained in first place. They were playing well, with the exception of Gil Hodges, who was hardly hitting at all. Reporters speculated that his new baby was responsible for his slump, causing him to stay up at night, making him continually exhausted and ten pounds lighter than he should be. I planned to write Hodges a letter of encouragement until I heard he was coming to Wolf's Sport Shop on Sunrise Highway that weekend to sign autographs. I had something that would surely help him break out of his slump and I wanted to give it to him personally.

Earlier that spring, while preparing for my Confirmation at religious-education classes in St. Agnes, I had entered a contest designed to test knowledge of the catechism. Actually, there were two contests, one among the parochial-school students and the other for students from public school. The winners in each group would then face off in a public competition. Every night after dinner, my mother would drill me in the articles of the Catholic faith. By the time the contest began, I felt unbeatable; I easily bested the others in my class and moved into a face-off with the champion from St. Agnes.

That night, I looked out from the stage to see my mother, a few friends, and an impressive array of white-clad nuns, the teachers of St. Agnes. The contest was modeled on a spelling bee. We would each be asked a question, and the first one who made a mistake would lose if the other contestant knew the answer. After several opening rounds, we were asked to take turns in naming the seven deadly sins. "Pride," my opponent called, and I responded, "Envy." "Lust," she rejoined with a smile, but I answered, "Covetousness." "Anger," she almost shouted. "Sloth," I almost whispered. Six sins down. Only one to go. For almost a minute my opponent stood in silence, rubbing her forehead in a gesture of intense thoughtfulness, while I, seeing her difficulty, felt a rising sense of exultant anticipation. "Deceit," she blurted out uncertainly. There was an audible sigh from the nuns in the audience. Now the moderator turned to me, and when I saw my mother confidently smiling in the audience I was unable to repress a grin of my own. "Gluttony," I announced in a confident tone, knowing the contest was won. Instead of an explosive cheer, what followed seemed to me a most unpleasant and protracted silence. In that momentary pause, I feared the nuns were disappointed that the girl from St. Agnes had not won, but the applause began and grew, and the Mother Superior seemed delighted when she presented me with my prize—a St. Christopher medal blessed by the Pope. Now this fruit of my triumph would help end the hitting slump of Gil Hodges.

Since St. Christopher was the patron saint of travel, my parents, like most Catholic families, always kept a St. Christopher medal in our car to protect the safety of our voyage. For years, I had heard my father threaten to affix a St. Christopher medal to our washing machine in order to ensure the safe return of every sock to its mate. If St. Christopher could protect socks and travelers, perhaps he could ensure the safe passage of Gil Hodges around the bases, preferably in one swing of the bat.

That weekend, not revealing my intentions, I asked my mother to drive me to Wolf's Sport Shop for my rendezvous with Gil Hodges. Slipping the small box from my pocket, I joined the line leading to Hodges, who looked uncomfortable, squeezed behind a small table. Nevertheless, he talked patiently to each person in turn, his manner warm and gracious. When I reached the head of the line, I handed him the small box, already opened to reveal the medal, and launched into an accompanying monologue. This medal has been blessed by the Pope, I explained, and I had won it in a catechism contest when I knew the seventh deadly sin was gluttony, and I thought St. Christopher would watch over his swing so that he could return home safely each time he went to bat, which would make him feel good and would make me feel good and would make Dodgers fans all over the world feel great. The people standing behind me greeted my rapid-fire message with good-natured laughter, but not Hodges. He accepted the medal with great solemnity. He told me that he, too, had once had a St. Christopher medal blessed by the Pope. But he had given it to his father, a coal miner in Indiana. Mining was a dangerous business, he explained, and his father had broken his back, lost an eye, and severed three toes in a series of accidents, so he thought his father needed the medal more than he did. He was thrilled, he said, to receive a medal of his own. He reached out in a gesture of gratitude, and my fingers disappeared in a palm four times the size of mine.

The next day, the Dodgers left for a long road trip, and Hodges began to hit. By the first week in June, he was leading the majors with seventeen home runs in forty-four games, three ahead of Babe Ruth's mark. Sportswriters attributed his miraculous resurrection to his ability to sleep soundly since leaving his infant at home. But I knew better.

Although the Dodgers stayed in first place throughout June, the Giants found their groove, winning game after game to climb into second place, only five games behind. The topic of conversation among Giant fans, however, was not the performance of the team, but the appearance of an astonishing young center fielder named Willie Mays. After coming to the majors at the end of May and going hitless in his first twelve at bats, Mays had caught on fire. Leo Durocher claimed he was the best rookie he had ever seen. Giant fans had fallen in love with him. Max and Joe could talk of nothing else. He had changed the chemistry of the entire team, they claimed. His enthusiasm was infectious, his fielding incomparable, and his swing reminiscent of Joe DiMaggio's. I had to admit they were right. He was one of the most exciting players I had ever seen. And my silent envy was magnified by the knowledge that Campanella had urged the Dodgers to sign him, but the scout who was sent to watch him play had reported that he couldn't hit a curveball!

SUMMER WAS our season of exploration. Elaine and I rode our bicycles everywhere, and the map of our world expanded each year—beyond our immediate neighborhood and school to the library and the church, past Woolworth's and the Fantasy Theatre in the center of town, to the expanse of Allen Field. We leaned our bikes against a tree while we wandered off to the

142

swings, where, scuffing our feet in the dirt, we exchanged reminiscences from the school year just past. For the first time it seemed we had our own stores of experience, our own short histories—not just baseball history or History with a capital "H."

No one tried to rein in our expeditions so long as we came home when we promised. It never occurred to us that something might happen to the bikes we left behind, even less that anything might happen to us. There was simply nothing to fear. No one in our town could remember the last time there had been a murder or even a violent crime. In 1951, the forty-six-member police force in Rockville Centre made only 139 arrests, the great majority for traffic violations and minor offenses. The great "law-and-order" controversy of the day was the movement to prohibit pinball machines, which, judging by the village report, had taken on the threatening overtones conveyed by pool tables in *The Music Man;* in the same report, the local guardians of moral probity asked that residents be restrained in their summer dress, pointing out that "apparel that may be proper at the beach is not always proper for public streets."

Though our parents let us play on the street, walk to school, or ride our bikes into the village center without trepidation, they were haunted by the sweeping fear that marked our summers year after year—the fear of polio, a disease which struck silently and seemingly at random. In the midst of play, a healthy child might be struck down by a blinding headache or a high fever, transformed within hours or days into a lifelong invalid. Although children were the principal victims, the disease struck adults from every walk of life, and had even crippled a president of the United States.

In the late forties and early fifties, polio moved toward epidemic proportions, striking more victims in the seven years between 1948 and 1955 than in the previous thirty years combined. In 1949, more than ten thousand cases were reported, a number which tripled in 1950 and would reach sixty thousand two years later. And since many cases were undoubtedly left unreported by parents, fearing the unknown hazards of hospital quarantine, the actual numbers were probably much higher.

Ignorance of how the disease was transmitted bred an anxiety verging on terror, as parents and medical scientists alike speculated whether it might be carried through the air or conducted by way of food or water. Perhaps it came from insects, or the shock of plunging from the warm summer air into cold water. Lack of understanding about the spread of polio created a vacuum which parents and editorialists filled with a thousand admonitions: avoid crowded places where you may be sneezed or coughed upon; beware of contacts in trains, buses, or boats; keep children away from strangers; avoid swimming in cold water; don't sit around in wet clothes; don't play to the point of getting overtired; avoid public drinking fountains; avoid using one another's pencils, whistles, handkerchiefs, utensils, food; burn or bury garbage not tightly covered; wash your hands before eating; call your doctor immediately if you've got a stiff neck, upset stomach, headache, sore throat, or unexplained fever.

Each of our mothers evolved her own rules. At the height of the polio scare, Mrs. Friedle forbade Elaine to go under the sprinkler unless the temperature was above ninety degrees. Mrs. Rust insisted that her children come in from the street an hour early at night. My mother had even more elaborate rules, her anxiety for me greatly intensified by the fact that my sister Charlotte had contracted polio when she was three years old. When the doctor confirmed that Charlotte and a neighboring boy had polio, my mother collapsed and suffered a miscarriage. The neighboring boy was sent to the contagious ward at Willard Parker Communicable Disease Hospital, but my parents decided to keep Charlotte at home with nurses around the clock. Although the boy ended up paralyzed, Charlotte escaped with a brace on her weakened left leg that came off before the year's end.

When the tallies of those stricken sharply increased, my mother placed all public swimming pools off limits, carefully circumscribing my movements beyond our neighborhood. I resisted rules which seemed arbitrary and unreasonable, since I, like most children, did not share my parents' fear of a disease which seemed remote. To me, it was inconceivable that anything might impair my own vitality. Sensing my resistance, wishing to make the danger more real, one hot day when I had been told to stay inside, my mother called me down to the television set to see a young boy imprisoned within an "iron lung," the gigantic machine that pumped his chest. "You don't want to spend the rest of your life in one of those, do you?" she asked. The thought was so alien, I refused to admit it to consciousness, but afterward, occasionally, in my dreams at night, I saw myself stretched out, trapped within the fearsome metal monster.

Forbidden to go to the beach by our parents, Elaine and I spent our afternoons sitting under the big maple tree on her front lawn. We lounged in the shade reading comics and books, and knitted multicolored squares in preparation for the day when they would miraculously fuse into a beautiful afghan. On afternoons when both the Dodgers and the Yankees were playing an afternoon game, we set our dueling radios on opposite sides of the blanket, the warm voice of Red Barber issuing from one end of the blanket, the harsh, tinny voice of Mel Allen from the other.

IF FEAR OF POLIO had curtailed my physical activity, the Brooklyn Dodgers liberated my spirit. In July 1951, the Dodgers won ten in a row. Almost every night I went to bed hoping that sleep would speed the hours toward morning, when, as soon as my eyes opened, I would race downstairs to read the newspaper account of the Dodger victory I had witnessed the day before. Nor was a single reading enough. Throughout the day I would return to the sports pages, always left in an honored place on the kitchen table, experiencing anew a game-winning home run, or a spectacular double play that had ended an enemy rally. I would stop before the entrance of the butcher shop, pausing to calm myself, anxious not to appear gloating at my friends' misfortune, before I entered to post the latest Dodger triumph on the wonderful bulletin board they had provided.

By the midseason All-Star break, the Dodgers had moved eight and a half games ahead of the Giants. Seven Dodgers, the largest contingent from any team in either league, were chosen for the All-Star game—Robinson and Campanella, Hodges and Snider, Reese and Newcombe and Roe. My satisfaction soared in the second week of August, when the Dodgers swept a three-game series with the Giants, stretching their lead to twelve and a half games. The television camera caught Leo Durocher sitting in the dugout at the end of the third game, his head bent over his knees, his body slumped in dejection. The Dodgers, on the other hand, were the very image of jubilation, smiling, laughing, slapping their teammates on the back, while thousands of fans cheered in exultation.

But then something snapped. Justified satisfaction yielded to arrogance, to excessive pride. I sat with my father as he read newspaper stories telling how a few of the victorious Dodgers had gone banging on the door to the Giants' locker room, shouting "The Giants are dead!" and "How do you like it now, Leo?" Other Dodgers joined in and soon a chorus was struck: "Roll out the barrel, we got the Giants on the run."

"Someone should have stopped them," my father said when he read about the unpleasant incident in the papers. "Where in the world was Dressen?" He shook his head in disgust. "You can't go on like that—gloating and taunting. Steal a team's dignity and they'll fight like the devil to get it back."

Excessive pride, I thought, one of the deadliest of the seven deadly sins...Perhaps if they all went to confession, things would be all right. But they weren't all Catholics. "I could pray for them myself," I suggested, but my father only smiled affectionately.

The following week, after the Dodgers' lead reached a season high of thirteen and a half games, the Giants began to play their best ball of the season. They played like a team reborn: hitters who were striking out with men on base began to come through in the clutch; pitchers who had lost their control with the game on the line began to throw strikes. It was at last, Giant fans exulted, the team whose prowess in spring training had so excited New Yorkers and stirred sportswriters to prophecies of glory. They quickly reeled off eleven consecutive victories, their longest winning streak since 1938, five years before I was born. They narrowed the Dodger lead from a comfortable two-digit margin to an alarming six games. Delirious Giant fans remained in their seats long after each win, savoring the community which victory had forged.

Invoking the power of ancient baseball superstition, Leo Durocher wore the same socks, shirt, and tie every day the streak lasted. Bobby Thomson refused to change his undershorts with their distinctive pattern of black ants. "He's got ants in the pants and games in the bag," wrote a poetic scribe. Closer to home, Max Kropf roamed the butcher shop wearing the same faded Giant cap from the time he arrived in the morning until closing time. "I even wear it to bed," he told me. And that gave me an idea.

I became convinced that the streak might end if I could somehow get Max to take off his hat. With accumulated allowances, I went to Wolf's Sport Shop and bought a new Giant hat, black with the orange logo. "Your team is doing so well I wanted to give you a present," I explained to Max. With a twinkle in his eye, Max thanked me but explained that he didn't want it ruined by the blood and grease of the butcher shop. Instead, he reassured me, as my heart began to fall, he would keep it in an honored place on his bedside table so he would constantly be reminded of my generosity. I nodded with pretended pleasure. Thus Max continued to wear his battered old cap, and the Giants kept winning until their streak had reached an astonishing sixteen games.

While the Giants played with abandon, the Dodgers were tight and jittery, swinging at bad balls and stranding too many men on base. Both Snider and Reese fell into a slump, Campanella was injured and Newcombe exhausted. By the third week of September, the Dodgers' once-formidable lead had shrunk to a thin margin of three games. There was, however, one bright ray of new hope—the pitching of my friend from Rockville Centre Night, Clem Labine.

At the end of August, Labine made his first major-league start, pitching a seven-hit, 3–1 victory over Cincinnati. He followed this performance with three straight victories in September. Everyone was talking about Clem Labine, who had emerged from obscurity to become the hope of the Dodgers. I pulled my two Labine autographs from my shoe box of baseball memorabilia. Never would I find a better opportunity for trading a Labine for a Robinson. Eddie Rust accepted my deal on the condition I throw in a Billy Cox and an Andy Pafko. I hesitated, not because it wasn't a good deal, but because I remembered how I had told Labine that I could trade him for a Robinson on even terms. But Eddie wouldn't reconsider. It was three for one, or nothing. Reluctantly, I agreed. We came to terms, but later that night, as I placed my signed Robinson card on my bedside table so I could look at it before going to sleep, I felt a twinge of guilt. I worried that my bad faith might bring bad luck to the young rookie.

And sure enough, the very next day, Clem Labine's star began to wane. In the first inning of his fifth major-league start, he lost control of his curveball and loaded the bases. Dressen saw that he was pitching from the stretch and directed him to take a full windup. Labine, feeling he had better control from the stretch, disobeyed Dressen's order. The next batter hit a grand slam. Furious at the insubordination of his young pitcher, Dressen not only pulled Labine from the game but withdrew him from the rotation. Though Labine later admitted that he had made a mistake in ignoring the manager, Dressen made an even larger error when he sat down his hottest pitcher in order to teach him what would prove one of the most ill-timed lessons in the history of the Dodger franchise. The decision probably cost the Dodgers at least one or two games, games which turned out to be decisive.

The Giants' incredible surge, twelve wins in their last thirteen games, thirty-seven of the last forty-four, reached a dramatic climax when they tied the Dodgers for first place with only one game left in the regular season. Once again, the entire season would come down to the final day. On the last Sunday in September, the Giants beat the Braves in Boston

3–2, and moved into sole possession of first place for the first time all season. Everything now depended on the outcome of the Dodgers' contest against the Philadelphia Phillies.

That afternoon the neighborhood was silent. The customary shouts of playing children, the friendly gossip of grown-ups gathered on front lawns, had all been stilled. As we gathered in my house to watch the game, my parents greeted the Greenes and their three children, my father laughing when he saw the entire family wearing caps of Dodger blue. Mr. Rust and Eddie entered, along with Elaine Friedle, whose Yankees had already clinched the American League pennant.

The game started disastrously. The Phillies took a 6–1 lead in the third, due in part to an error by Robinson, who had struck out and hit into a double play in his first two trips at bat. In the fifth inning, it was Robinson again, this time as hero. He sent a triple to the wall which drove in one run, and then he scored a second run himself a few minutes later. In the eighth, the Dodgers scored three more runs, and the ninth inning ended with the game tied.

In the bottom of the twelfth inning, with two outs, the Phillies loaded the bases. Devastation was only ninety feet away. Then Eddie Waitkus hit a screaming line drive over second base. Robinson raced to his right, dove, and lay sprawled on the ground. As the baserunner on third raced toward the plate, the umpire ran toward the prostrate Robinson, saw the ball in his glove, and jerked his thumb skyward, signaling that the inning was over. The crowd in Philadelphia, which had been on its feet, fell silent, but my house exploded in celebration.

The cameras followed Robinson as he was helped back to the dugout, where he sat slumped on the bench. The Dodger trainer held a piece of cotton soaked in ammonia under his nose. The announcers told us that he probably wouldn't be able to stay in the game. "Push him out there, Doc," Reese yelled. "He'll be all right once he gets on the field." And after the Dodgers failed to score in the top of the thirteenth, there he was, standing right beside second.

I sat tense and silent as the Phillies came to bat. I always hated it when the other team was up at bat, but this was far worse than usual. Seeing my anxiety, my father tried to comfort me. "I know," he said, "nothing's worse than extra innings played on the other team's field. One swing can end it all." I wasn't comforted. That was the whole point.

In the top of the fourteenth inning, the game still tied, with two outs, the mighty Robinson came to bat. "C'mon, Robby," I urged, "you can do it. I know you can"—and then, flatteringly, "you always do." I tried to summon all my strength and send it through the television set. Robinson wheeled on the pitch and drove an immense home run into the bleachers that would win the game and send the Dodgers into a three-game playoff for the championship of the National League.

We had done it. We all raced out into the street. Grown men were slapping neighbors on the back, pumping each other's hands, as if they had just received an award.

That night, cheering crowds greeted both the Giants and the Dodgers as their respective trains converged on New York. "I've seen a lot of ball games in my time," Dodger pitching coach Clyde Sukeforth said as he stood on the platform, "but I've never seen a greater one."

It was the second-most-dramatic moment of the 1951 season. The most memorable was yet to come.

THE COMPLETION of a continental cable a few months earlier had made possible the first national audience for any sporting event. Thus baseball enthusiasts from all over America were watching as more than thirty thousand fans crowded Ebbets Field for the opening game of the playoffs, to see home runs by Bobby Thomson and Monte Irvin give the Giants a 3–1 victory. The next day, at the Polo Grounds, his pitching staff exhausted by the ordeal of the closing weeks, Dressen called on Clem Labine, who pitched a brilliant six-hit, 10–0 shutout in the biggest game of his career. In the *Daily News* the next morning, I saw a picture of a smiling Dressen, his arm draped around the young rookie hurler. I couldn't help imagining how things might have turned out if Dressen hadn't put Labine into the doghouse two weeks earlier.

October 3, 1951, was unseasonably warm, more like summer than early fall. When I returned home for lunch, both my sisters had already arrived, having left the city so they might watch the big game with my mother. Jeanne had graduated from high school with high honors the previous June and had followed Charlotte into the nursing program at Lenox Hill. Despite Charlotte's claim that she had been drawn to nursing for its starched white uniforms, she had already become an exceptional nurse. At the age of twenty-four, she was the head nurse on the evening shift of the male surgical ward. Her tough, no-nonsense supervision of the nursing staff had earned her the nickname "Stonewall Jackson."

When I implored my mother to let me remain at home after lunch, she agreed without hesitation. "Of course," she said. What other decision was possible? Our teachers had let us listen to the first two games on the radio. But I badly wanted to watch this culminating game. And I wanted to be in the sanctity of my home, sitting on the couch, my scorebook across my lap. Later, I discovered that more than half my classmates had failed to return to school that afternoon.

Each team had saved its best for last—Sal Maglie against Don Newcombe, both twenty-game winners. For seven innings, they battled to a 1–1 tie. It was the worst kind of stressful game. Then, in the top of the eighth, after a Duke Snider single sent Pee Wee Reese to third, the fearsome Maglie threw a sharp breaking curve which soared past both Robinson and his own catcher. Reese scored and the Dodgers were ahead. "It serves the old beanballer right!" I said. Now, with a man on second, hoping to set up a double play, Durocher ordered Maglie to walk Robinson. But the next batter, Billy Cox singled, both runners scored, and the Dodgers were ahead 4–1. Quickly, I turned to my scorebook and meticulously drew the lines which told the story, anxious to inscribe the glorious moment for enduring history.

In the eighth inning, a visibly tiring Newcombe pitched himself out of a jam, and the score was still 4–1 as the game entered the bottom of the ninth. "Three more outs," I prayed silently, "just give us three more outs." And even though I always feared the worst in the most gloomy depths of my imagination, I could never have conceived what was to come.

After Alvin Dark led off with a single, Don Mueller hit a bouncing ground ball up the middle, sending Dark to third. With one out, Whitey Lockman hit a solid double, scoring Dark and sending Mueller to third, where he collapsed on the base path, having caught his spike on the base. All eyes were focused on the stricken Mueller, who, grimacing in pain, was lifted onto a stretcher. Almost unnoticed, Chuck Dressen left the dugout and strode purposefully to the mound. "Oh, no,"

I exclaimed involuntarily. "Newk will come through. Leave him in."

"He's had it," disagreed my mother. "Bring on Erskine." But it was Ralph Branca who began the long walk to the pitching mound. I was horrified. Images of Branca's other failures filled my mind—his reputation for giving up hits in tight situations, the home-run balls he had pitched to Bobby Thomson and Monte Irvin in the first game. "No, no," I whispered, addressing my entreaties to the empty, indifferent air, "please send him back; anybody but Branca."

But my pleas were fruitless. The stage was set, the moment irrevocable. Ralph Branca stood on the mound, the destiny of millions in his hands. And Bobby Thomson was advancing to the plate.

"Don't worry," Jeanne said to me. "Everything's going to work out."

"This is it," announced Charlotte. "He's going to hit a homer right now and win it for the Giants."

Almost instantly, before I could even feel angry, my hands clenched, my body rigid, I saw Thomson swing. Then came the never-to-be-forgotten voice of Giant announcer Russ Hodges. "There's a long fly....It's gonna be...I believe." He stopped for a moment. Then, as the ball dropped majestically into the lower deck of seats, there came that horrifying shout. "The Giants win the pennant! The Giants win the pennant! The Giants win the pennant!"

I threw down my scorebook, the last page never to be completed. For a moment I believed that my sister's prophecy had influenced the outcome and I hated her with all my heart. That night and the following day, I couldn't bear to talk about the game, nor did I read the papers the following day, though I did catch a glimpse of Branca stretched out alone on the clubhouse steps. I was told that he couldn't stop crying, repeating over and over, "Why me, why me?"

It was the worst moment in my life as a fan, worse even than any loss to the Yankees in the World Series, and clearly I was not alone. From that moment to this, Bobby Thomson and the Brooklyn Dodgers would be forever linked, the mere mention of his name calling forth in every Dodger fan instant recognition, comradeship, a memory of where they were, how they felt. I now live in the town of Concord, Massachusetts, not far from the Old North Bridge, where the American Revolution began. Whenever I take visitors to see the monument, and stand before the marble shaft, reading that lovely inscription which commemorates "the shot heard round the world," I think privately of Bobby Thomson's home run.

Despondent and humiliated, I could not make myself return to the butcher shop to complete the last entry on the Bryn Mawr bulletin board. When walking to and from school, I would cross to the opposite side of the street so they couldn't see me. After almost a week had passed, a large bouquet of red roses arrived at my door addressed to me. It was the first time anyone had sent me flowers.

"Ragmop, please come back," the card read. "We miss you. Your friends at the Bryn Mawr Meat Market."

My excitement about the flowers drowned my humiliation and pain over the Dodgers' collapse. I ran to the store to thank them, and while I was there, I took a deep breath and made the final entry.

CHAPTER FIVE

My first exposure to the Cold War that dominated American politics in the decades after World War II came through the disheveled figure of Whittaker Chambers, the most notorious alumnus in the history of South Side Senior High School in Rockville Centre. Chambers' sensational accusation that a high-ranking State Department official, the patrician and greatly respected Alger Hiss, had spied for the Soviet Union, catapulted him into the national spotlight. Chambers went on to provide the House Committee on Un-American Activities with the names of other government officials who, he alleged, had secretly served the Soviet Union. His testimony helped inaugurate a search for traitors in our midst; and, not incidentally, gave an enormous boost to the political career of

Richard Nixon, who, like John Kennedy of Massachusetts, was a war veteran serving his second term in Congress.

However one felt about Chambers, and judgment was seriously divided, he had become the most controversial of our local citizens. Memories were searched for tales from his boyhood, for the origins, as it were, of this traitor turned patriot. He had, according to rumor, made a suicide pact with his brother Dick, but after Dick had killed himself, Chambers reneged on his end of the deal. Later, he scandalized our area of Long Island by bringing a woman of "low repute" to live in his mother's house. Although I heard these stories and more, the only one that hit home was the tale of his outrageous class-day address—a story I first heard while listening to my sister and her friends discuss the graduation oration which Jeanne had been chosen to deliver.

"I'm going to pull a Chambers," Jeanne asserted.

"What's a Chambers?" I asked.

Some thirty years ago, Jeanne's friends explained, Chambers had been selected by his classmates to compose a class prophecy. When he submitted his speech to the principal for required approval, his cynical, vituperative remarks were deemed inappropriate. Unless he changed them, he would not be allowed to speak. He made the required revisions, but on the appointed day, he reverted to his original speech, which, among other unsavory passages, predicted a career in prostitution for one of his classmates. Angry school officials forbade him to attend the graduation ceremony the next day. They withheld his diploma until the middle of the summer, when his distraught mother, arguing that his artistic temperament had gotten the better of him, finally persuaded them to release it.

Jeanne's friends explained that it was a great tradition to follow Chambers, that it was Jeanne's responsibility to deliver a perverse speech—to tell her classmates that they should aim low rather than high, follow their self-interest rather than their ideals, be ready to snitch on their closest friends if it would help them to get ahead.

"You'd never do that, would you?" I asked, not liking the whole business one bit, but Jeanne and her friends simply smiled. By the time Jeanne stood up to deliver her speech on the theme "So Much to Remember," I was anything but relaxed. As soon as she began to speak, however, I realized that they had been teasing me. Jeanne delivered an idealistic speech, and received a warm welcome from the audience. I was so relieved that I couldn't even remember to be annoyed. But, clearly, Chambers had left his mark in our small world, his name connoting unimaginable transgressions.

In the larger world, the apprehension that communist subversion was undermining America, heightened by Chambers' disclosures, was intensified enormously by news that the

Soviet Union had exploded an atomic bomb. It seemed inconceivable to many that the Russians had mastered nuclear science on their own. Traitorous spies must have provided the secret. The search for communist sympathizers in the government spiraled into a nationwide hysteria.

Now that America no longer had a monopoly over nuclear weapons, the devastating power which had brought the Japanese to their knees might be turned against us. The threat of an atomic attack not only changed the course of the Cold War; it produced reactions which filtered down from the offices of government into the lives of an entire generation of young people. To us, the Cold War was not an abstraction. It was the air-raid drills in school, the call for bomb shelters, and exposure to the deliberately unsettling horror of civil-defense films. Our generation was the first to live with the knowledge that, in a single instant, everyone and everything we knew—our family, our friends, our block, our world—could be brought to an end. If a bomb exploded in Manhattan, which was considered a likely target, its fireball would vaporize everything from Central Park to Washington Square, and produce deadly fallout over a twenty-to-thirty-mile radius. On the basis of some obscure calculation, we were informed that the bomb's impact would reach Rockville Centre in twelve minutes.

The air-raid drills conducted by our school were treated with the utmost seriousness.

When the shriek of sirens interrupted our studies, we practiced two different drills. On the assumption that the bomb was close by, we were to fall to the floor, face down beneath our desks, elbows over our heads, eyes shut. Although I could never figure out how my flimsy desk, with its worn inkwell and its years of name-scratching, could protect me from the atomic bomb, I did what I was told, and kept absolutely still while we awaited the shriek of the falling missile. In the second drill, designed for situations in which there was time to take cover, teachers led us into the hallway and down into the basement, where they directed us to lean against the wall and fold our arms over our heads.

We were told to practice the first drill—the one which anticipated an imminent explosion—at our homes at night, so we would be prepared to fall out of bed and onto the floor with maximum speed. Between these practice "atomic fallings," and the hundreds of prayers I said each night for my own account, for the poor souls in purgatory, and for my family and the Dodgers, it is a wonder that I ever got to sleep.

My Catholic faith provided one peculiar benefit to offset the possible destruction of the entire world in a nuclear holocaust. I had always assumed that my afterlife would require many restless years in purgatory before I was lifted into heaven. If my death coincided with the last day of the world, however, there would be no layover in purgatory, for on that last day, we were taught, Christ would pass a General Judgment on all the men, women, and children who had ever lived, sentencing each person either to heaven or to hell.

But what if the bomb fell, whole cities were destroyed, and yet some people survived? Though we understood there was no hope of living if the bomb fell directly on our village, the civil-defense authorities optimistically assured us that, with twelve minutes' warning and with efficient civil-defense mechanisms in place, the casualties in our city could be reduced by 50 percent. I remember seeing a film in school: *How Can You Stay Alive in an Atom Bomb Blast?* The narrator described a self-contained underground shelter which could be built in your backyard for less than two thousand dollars. More practical for most people was the film's suggestion that an existing basement could be converted into a shelter, and stocked with canned foods, soft drinks, candles, and a first-aid kit. The film also extolled the importance of civil-defense volunteers, who would assume all manner of responsibilities in case of an attack, serving as air-raid wardens and auxiliary policemen, and directing people to emergency shelters.

At regular intervals, the entire town participated in what were called "Atom Attack Tests." All pedestrian and vehicular traffic was brought to a halt when the siren rang. Thousands of volunteers were mobilized, including Boy Scouts and high-school seniors, to act the role of casualties and evacuees.

Victims were carried to emergency hospitals; makeshift shelters were supplied with cots and blankets. In one location, volunteer firemen fought to subdue a blazing pit of oil, nearly blinded by thick "smoke" provided by a fog machine that belonged to the Public Works Mosquito Division. Others fought a simulated apartment-fire without the aid of water, on the assumption that an atomic blast would put the water mains out of service. The films and demonstrations were not meant to frighten us, we were told, but to prepare us. No amount of preparation, however, could hide the gruesome fact that an atomic bomb would kill tens of thousands of people, and, as the leader of the Soviet Union, Nikita Khrushchev, would later express it: "The living would envy the dead."

Not wanting to dwell on such macabre thoughts, I concentrated on how to find a safe and pleasant shelter for my family and my friends, one that we could reach in the space of twelve minutes. To my mind, my own basement was terribly inadequate. It didn't offer even the makings of a proper shelter. No matter how many cans of food we stockpiled there, it remained an unfinished room with no rug on the concrete floor and no couches or chairs. The room contained little besides an old Ping-Pong table, my father's tools, and our Bendix washer with its clear glass face that allowed you to watch the clothes tumbling through the cycles. I did not think I could tolerate staring at that washer, week after week.

The Friedles' finished basement was much more inviting, but I worried that it wasn't big enough to accommodate our family along with all the Friedles.

My solution was just around the corner. One day, when shopping for my mother in the delicatessen, I accompanied Mrs. Probst to the basement to find a cardboard box that my mother needed for storage. The staircase led us into a large room stocked with hundreds of cans of food and supplies. As we crossed the room to pick up an empty box, I saw a metal door at the far end of the darkened basement. I questioned Mrs. Probst and she explained that on the other side of the door was the basement of the soda shop, and that all the stores were connected. Instantly, I envisioned all the doors flung open, creating one block-long rectangular space which provided access to the stores and supplies above, and could accommodate our entire neighborhood below. Everything was there. With Doc Schimmenti as our resident physician, we could use the supplies in the drugstore to set up a makeshift infirmary, complete with Band-Aids, Ace bandages, and all sorts of drugs and medicines. The rack of best-sellers would provide reading material, supplemented by the magazines and comic books from both the drugstore and the soda shop. Canned peas, string beans, tuna fish, peanut butter, and soups would be available from the delicatessen. In a pinch, the huge burlap bags filled with sawdust beneath the butcher shop could provide bedding.

This was too big an idea to keep to myself. Before the afternoon was over, I had visited every store to explain how, once the siren sounded, we could set in motion a system whereby we all worked together to move everything we needed into the connecting basements as quickly as possible. I volunteered to inform the entire neighborhood of the unique opportunity that was available and how best to utilize it. Mrs. Probst nodded approvingly, and Doc Schimmenti patted me on the head.

Later that afternoon, I stopped in the butcher shop to ask Max and Joe if I could leave a few things in the corner of their basement so I'd be ready to move in when the bomb fell. I planned to store my baseball cards, a Monopoly board, a box of my favorite books, and, most important, my collection of scorebooks from previous years. If we were trapped for days or even weeks, I could entertain everyone by re-creating virtually every Dodger game that had been played over the past few seasons. Although the butchers endorsed my plan, they convinced me that it was unnecessary to implement it immediately, and furthermore suggested that, instead of carting my belongings to their dusty basement, I should keep everything I wanted in a suitcase under my bed, in readiness for transport to the connecting basements should the siren ring. This made more sense than my idea, for I wouldn't have to part with my beloved possessions. They would always be right under my bed, ready for immediate flight.

Now that I had formulated a reasonable plan for the evacuation that would allow me, my family, and our entire neighborhood not only to survive the bomb but to flourish intact in our subterranean shelter, I was ready to resume ordinary life.

ON THE JUNE DAY in 1950 when the Korean War began, the summer's first heat wave had sent temperatures into the nineties. I was sitting with my parents on the porch in front of an old General Electric fan when the radio reported that North Korea had invaded South Korea. My most vivid memory is the whirring sound of that fan and the anxious faces of my parents.

My sisters recalled in detail the world map that hung on the wall of our breakfast nook during World War II. It came with a set of pins which my father would move every few days to mark the position of the American troops. But there was no equivalent map to trace the course of battle in Korea. I had very little awareness of the events in what would later become known as the "forgotten war." It seemed to have very little to do with me. If I knew about the spectacular parade honoring the return of General Douglas MacArthur in April 1951, it was largely because the procession delayed the opening game of the first series between the Dodgers and the Giants, thus allowing me time to get home from school and watch most of the game.

Although I thought of myself as a patriot, my heart full of pride each morning as I recited the ritual phrases of the pledge to the flag, the tragedy of war seemed real to me only when it directly affected the fortunes of the Brooklyn Dodgers. For three years, Don Newcombe had been our best and most consistent pitcher, with seventeen victories in his rookie year, nineteen the next year, and twenty the year after. Only Warren Spahn of the Braves had won more games during that period. Then, in 1952, at the height of his powers, the twenty-six-year-old Newcombe was drafted into the army. Other teams suffered losses just as great—the Yankees lost Whitey Ford, the Giants Willie Mays, and the Red Sox Ted Williams—but the only thing that concerned me was Dressen's ability to compensate for the loss of Newcombe.

The summer of 1952 was one of the hottest New Yorkers had ever experienced. Day after day, the temperature stayed in the high nineties. Under the strain of the heat wave, flowers wilted and tempers flared. At night, the small electric fan at the foot of my bed only circulated the heat. Unable to jump rope or play hopscotch on the steaming sidewalks, Elaine and I conceived a plan to make the best of the heat: we would read *Gone with the Wind*. We sat in the shade of the large maple tree on Elaine's lawn and let the story of Scarlett O'Hara and Rhett Butler absorb our imaginations and distract us from the scorched brown lawns of that blistering summer. Vicariously, we lived the great romance. Elaine identified with the gentle decency of Melanie Wilkes; I preferred the shrewd strength of the outspoken Scarlett. We both fell for the unscrupulous Rhett with his dancing dark eyes and his white Panama hat. We were both titillated when, during the Siege of Atlanta, Rhett asked Scarlett to live with him. Expecting a proposal of matrimony, Scarlett is furious: "Mistress!" she snaps. "What would I get out of that except a passel of brats?" We parsed the sentence as if it were a passage from the Bible. What exactly did she mean?

The summer was almost over when we reached the final pages. Devastated by Rhett's rejection of Scarlett in the final scene, I could not accept his argument that "what is broken is broken," that it was too late to glue together the fragments of their love. I ran into my house to ask my mother what she thought.

"She'll get him back, won't she?" I asked. "Once she gets to Tara, she'll figure out some way, won't she?"

"No," she said softly, "I don't think so. Maybe Scarlett could have reached out to Rhett when the little girl died, but by the end, it was too late."

Disconsolate, I ran up to my room. There I began to imagine, complete with dialogue, ways in which I might help bring about a reconciliation.

The fictional romance of Scarlett and Rhett occupied my imagination, but my sister Charlotte was involved in a romantic adventure of her own. While working the night shift at Lenox Hill, she had met a young intern, Dr. Paul Ovando. When he first saw her picture in the hospital yearbook, he told her he had decided that she would one day become his wife. Charlotte scoffed at his presumption, but within weeks she had fallen in love and they were making marriage plans. Both families felt it was too soon for them to marry. Paul had just finished his internship, and was scheduled to start five years of surgical residency at Mary Hitchcock Hospital in Hanover, New Hampshire. Once the residency was completed, he faced specialized training in thoracic surgery. It seemed better, both sets of parents agreed, to postpone marriage until he was further advanced. Unwilling to accept delay, Charlotte and Paul eloped in the summer of '52. I couldn't understand how they could marry without a proper wedding, but their decision to run away together seemed enviably romantic and only served to fix Charlotte's glamorous image in my mind.

With my mind aswirl with hazy ideas of love and romance, the fictional mingling with the actual, the friendship I rekindled with Johnny that summer acquired new possibilities. I hadn't seen him much the previous two summers, because he had gone to sleepaway camp, but during the summer of '52, he had returned to Jones Beach. He was now eleven and at least six inches taller than I. We resumed our conversations about baseball, but our relationship was not as relaxed as it had once been. Though he always seemed glad to see me, he was given to occasional bouts of teasing. After talking for a few minutes, he would sometimes shove me under water and swim away. I would come up coughing, irritated, and perplexed. To my amazement, Jeanne explained that his behavior meant he liked me.

One afternoon, after a long talk about how well the Dodgers were doing, Johnny mentioned that he was returning to Jones Beach that night with his older brother to see the musical production of *A Night in Venice* at the new outdoor theater.

"So am I," I said. "With my sister."

"Well, look for me," he mumbled, "and we'll sit together."

Jones Beach was a different world at night, its dazzling colors softened, the menacing heat of the day diminished by a cool breeze. The new outdoor theater, a semicircular shell of brick and concrete on Zach's Bay, was capable of seating over eight thousand people. Michael Todd's production of the musical extravaganza *A Night in Venice* featured a cast of three hundred, including singers from the Metropolitan Opera Company, a fifty-piece orchestra, singing gondoliers, precision swimmers, and world-famous divers, performing spectacular stunts off three diving boards at once.

Johnny was waiting for me when I walked in, his hair slicked back and his plaid shirt rolled up at the elbows. I felt shy and didn't say much as we found seats together. At one point in the water ballet, as the music of Johann Strauss floated across the water, Johnny brushed my hand and pointed to the precision swimmers seated atop a huge lotus blossom that had suddenly risen from the bottom of the lagoon. He quickly withdrew his hand, but his brief contact had unaccountably delighted me.

The next morning I couldn't wait to get back to Jones Beach, but, to my dismay, the papers were filled with reports of a new polio outbreak. None of us were allowed to go to the beach. My mother's ban remained in force for nearly two weeks. Immediately upon my return, I looked for Johnny. I couldn't find him, and on the days following, my luck proved no better. I searched the boardwalk, the ice-cream parlors, the pitch-and-putt golf course without result. I wondered if he was trying to avoid me.

The summer came to an end and I never saw Johnny again, but in my mind, he became the leading man in a daydream I invented and elaborated upon. To explain his absence, I imagined that he had become a polio victim and that I was his loving caretaker, pushing his wheelchair along the boardwalk at the beach where we had once run together, propelling him up the ramp at Ebbets Field to share the World Series victory we had both desired for so long. Exactly how the summer heat, my sister's elopement, my fear of polio, and my reading of *Gone with the Wind* came together I wasn't sure, but the combination provided all the ingredients necessary to yield the pleasures and pains of the first full-blown imagined romance of my life.

AN OVERHEARD ARGUMENT between Mr. Friedle and my father constitutes my only clear recollection of the presidential election of 1952. My family almost never discussed politics. As a civil servant, my father never involved himself in individual campaigns; but in '52, with the fight for the Republican nomination under way, he declared his support for Dwight Eisenhower. Mr. Friedle argued that Robert Taft was Mr. Republican, a loyal member of the party whose conservative ideals had remained consistent for dozens of years. Eisenhower, he asserted, had no political identity, and could as easily have been a Democrat as a Republican. "That's exactly why I'm for him," my father replied. "We need a rest from all the bickering of the last few years. We need a healer, a man above politics. Ike is that man."

As the presidential election approached, the Dodgers won four games in a row to clinch the National League pennant. Three days later, the Yankees won the American League pennant by defeating second-place Cleveland. October would bring the fourth World Series between the two New York teams.

"The simplest argument to support a belief that the Yankees will win," Red Smith stated in the *Tribune,* "is to point out that they always do. Since the beginning of time, no Brooklyn team has won a world championship....It does not, of course, follow that what has always happened in the past must of necessity continue to happen. Yet one suspects that the knowledge of what has always happened must have some effect upon the players and the games."

"I see that I've got blue-green eyes because you've got blue-green eyes," I protested to my father, "but I don't see how a team can lose because it lost five or ten or twenty years ago. That doesn't make any sense." My father explained that a team's legend had staying power beyond the individual players; that, as newcomers join the club, they trade tales of the past, just as citizens absorb the legends of their country. When the stories tell of great achievement, as the Yankees' did, each new player absorbs the confidence of his elders. In reverse fashion, if a new Dodger player repeatedly hears how his team has lost every World Series, he begins to think, as soon as something goes wrong, that once again the team is going to lose.

However, my father quickly added that, although this was generally true, it did not apply to this particular Dodger team, which was the best and proudest of all Dodger teams in his lifetime. Certainly, he reassured me, players like Robinson and Reese and Campanella would not be influenced by past defeats and would be spurred to win their first World Series.

The Dodgers won the first game, 4–2, on the arm of Joe Black, the Negro League star whose brilliant pitching in the bullpen would earn him Rookie of the Year honors. It was the first time, Red Smith quipped, "since the dawn of civilization that Brooklyn won a series opener." The Yankees tied the Series in the second game with a three-hitter by Vic Raschi and a three-run homer by Elaine's idol, Billy Martin. The Dodgers won the third game behind Preacher Roe; the Yankees took the fourth, 2–0, with a home run by their twenty-year-old golden boy, Mickey Mantle. In the fifth and most exciting game, the Dodgers pulled out a 6–5 victory in the eleventh inning. Ahead three games to two, we needed only one more victory. But the Yankees tied the Series with a sixth-game victory when both Mantle and Berra hit home runs.

The world championship was decided in the seventh inning of the seventh game. With the Yankees ahead by a score of 4–2, and two out, the Dodgers loaded the bases for Robinson. After running the count to three and two, Robinson hit a twisting pop fly which the gusting wind carried to the first-base side of the pitcher's mound. As the Yankee pitcher, Bob Kuzava, stood frozen on the mound, and first baseman Joe Collins lost the ball in the sun, the Dodgers began to round the bases, until Billy Martin, realizing what had happened, raced the distance from second base, lunged through the air, and caught the ball just before it hit the ground. Martin's spectacular catch ended the Dodger rally, and the Yankees went on to win the game and the Series, their fourth championship in a row.

As soon as the game was over, Elaine strutted to the entrance of my house. "You have absolutely nothing to be ashamed of," she magnanimously consoled me, "nothing at all. It could just as easily have gone your way and almost did." She tried to suppress a smile. "You gave us a real run for..." I couldn't bear to hear another word. I closed the door in her face and ran up to my room.

ALTHOUGH MY INTEREST in public events rarely went beyond the sports pages, I became absorbed by the story of Julius and Ethel Rosenberg, arrested for divulging atomic secrets to the Soviet Union. Their trial, conviction, and death sentence, in the spring and summer of 1953, provided front-page stories month after month.

Brief clips on television and in newspaper photographs made the Rosenbergs appear disturbingly familiar. The short, plump Mrs.

Rosenberg looked more like one of my friends' mothers than an international spy. A photo of the Rosenberg boys showed the older boy, Michael, who was exactly my age, with his arm around his five-year-old brother, Robert, walking along a barbed-wire fence after visiting their parents in jail. They could have been among my playmates on the block. They had "a fine time," the article reported, running up and down the corridors of the jail. But they didn't seem happy to me. Whenever I ate Jell-O, my favorite dessert, I was reminded of the Rosenbergs. Julius Rosenberg had reportedly torn a Jell-O box in two, giving one half to his brother-in-law, David Greenglass, who was stationed at Los Alamos, where the atomic bomb was built, and the other half to Harry Gold, a now confessed Soviet spy, so the two men could identify one another.

Though the majority of our neighborhood families believed the Rosenbergs guilty, opinion was divided on whether the death penalty was appropriate. Proponents of execution agreed with Judge Irving Kaufman that, by "putting into the hands of the Russians the A-bomb before our best scientists predicted Russia would perfect the bomb," the Rosenbergs were responsible for the Korean War and for the sense of doom that hung over every American. "By your betrayal, you have altered the course of history," Kaufman told Julius and Ethel Rosenberg when he sentenced them to death. Opponents of execution believed the husband and wife were too unsophisticated to hold key positions in the spy ring and pointed to the more lenient sentences meted out to all the others involved: fourteen years for physicist Klaus Fuchs, who had been a member of the Los Alamos inner circle and had turned over atomic secrets to the Soviet Union; thirty for the courier, Harry Gold; fifteen for Ethel's brother, David Greenglass, and no prosecution for Ruth Greenglass, David's wife. Was the discrepancy simply, they speculated, because the Rosenbergs had refused to admit their guilt?

For the Jewish families on our block, it was a particularly awkward and stressful time. Mrs. Lubar later revealed her shame that the Rosenbergs were Jewish, although she also felt sorry for them and didn't think they should be executed. More conservative Jews seemed anxious to display their patriotism by vocal denunciations of the Rosenbergs. Still others distanced themselves from the entire case, fearing that discussion would trigger an anti-Semitic backlash.

I didn't know who was right, about either the crime —or the penalty. All I knew was that some huge and incomprehensible force had reached out to devastate this very ordinary-appearing family. When I read that young Michael had learned that his parents were about to be executed while he was watching a Yankees-Tigers game on television, I tried to imagine what it would be like having a bulletin break up the order of a public baseball game with such crushing private news. To me, all the arguments among our neighbors meant less than the sight of young Michael in tears, confronting the loss of his parents. Michael was not only the same age as I, but the same age my father had been when both his parents had died. Surely the Rosenbergs would break down at the last minute and agree to talk in exchange for their lives, so that Michael and Robert wouldn't be abandoned. My mother was less certain. "They see themselves as martyrs," she explained. "They will never crack." My mother was right. "We are innocent," Ethel insisted right up to the end. "This is the whole truth. To forsake this truth is to pay too high a price even for the priceless gift of life—for life thus purchased we could not live out in dignity and self-respect."

It was hot and humid in New York on the night of Friday, June 19, 1953. The time of the executions, originally set for 11 P.M., had been moved up so they would not fall on the Jewish Sabbath. Around 8:15 P.M., radio and television shows were interrupted by the announcement that the Rosenbergs were dead. I wondered what kind of life the two children would lead and where they would go to school. I hoped Michael Rosenberg would take care of his little brother, just as my father had cared for his sister, Marguerite, when they, too, were orphaned. My reverie was broken by the insistent bleat and blare of horns as dozens of motorists cruising the streets honked their approval of the executions.

For days afterward, Elaine and I followed

the story of the executions in the newspapers and on television with a ghoulish fascination. Julius, without his spectacles and with his mustache shaved off, had been the first to enter the death chamber. He was strapped into the chair, the switch was pulled, and a buzzing sound filled the room. Two more shocks were applied before he was pronounced dead.

Next, wearing a dark-green dress with white polka dots, Michael's mother, Ethel, entered the room. As she reached the chair, she turned and embraced the matron, who choked up and left the room. The guards dropped the leather mask over her face. The first of the three standard shocks was applied at 8:11. "She seemed to fight death," *The New York Times* reported. "She strained hard against the straps and her neck turned red. A thin column of grayish smoke rose from the upper side of her head. Her hands, lying limp, were now clenched like a fighter's." After the standard three shocks of electricity, one short and two long, doctors approached to check her heartbeat and discovered that Ethel was still alive. Her straps were readjusted and a fourth shock was applied. Once more, she strained against the straps. A fifth current was required before the doctors pronounced her dead.

"He was so meek," a neighbor said later, "it took only a few minutes to kill him, but she was so tough, it took forever to kill her. Proves she was the mastermind behind the whole thing."

AT THE END OF THE SUMMER, Eddie and Eileen's parents, Julia and Arthur Rust, invited all the neighbors on the block to attend a party and watch movies of their trip to Ireland. My favorite priest, Father O'Farrell, was there, along with two doctors and about a dozen children. My mother was seated on a stool watching the movies when I noticed that she was flushed. She kept pressing her fingers against the sides of her forehead, as if to squeeze away the pain of a headache. Suddenly, and without warning, she slumped from the stool to the floor. The doctors rushed to her side while Julia Rust called the fire department. The adults tried to get the children out of the house, but I refused to budge. I overheard a doctor say that my mother had suffered a major heart attack and her condition was critical. "We should think about last rites," one of the doctors said to Father O'Farrell. "No, no," I cried out, afraid they were accepting my mother's death. "You can't, I won't let you." Father O'Farrell put his hand gently on my shoulder. The anointing of the sick, he reassured me, was a sacrament to give strength not only to the soul but to the body.

My father, accompanied by my sister Jeanne, who was home from nursing school for the weekend, went with my mother in the ambulance to Mercy Hospital, a few miles away. When I tried to join them, my father told me with uncharacteristic abruptness that I couldn't come. As soon as they had left, Julia Rust told Eileen to take a walk with me. We circled the block aimlessly, round and round, until we settled into my house to wait. I sat with Eileen in front of the television set, brief periods of conversation alternating with periods of silence, as I pretended to watch television. Neither of us discussed what had happened. Around midnight, my father finally came home to report that my mother was in an oxygen tent and that Jeanne was staying with her.

It was fortunate Jeanne was there that night. She knew that my mother could not tolerate heat; all summer she had kept a big fan by her chair and her bed. "It's impossible in this tent," my mother kept saying. "It's unbearably hot." Jeanne checked the tent and discovered that there was no oxygen left. When she ran to the nurses' station with the information, she was told that more oxygen had been ordered and would arrive in several hours. "Let's take her out of the tent until then," my sister suggested. "There's more oxygen outside than in that stifling tent."

"Can't do that," the nurse responded. "The doctor ordered an oxygen tent for her, so we've got to keep her there until we get a second order."

"That's crazy," my sister argued, as she unzipped the plastic sides of the tent and started moving Mother. The nurse resisted, but Jeanne promptly silenced the nurse's protests. "Listen," she ordered. "I'm taking her out of this tent and she will remain outside until the oxygen arrives. That's all there is to it."

This incident was my mother's fourth hospitalization in three years. In 1950, she had been hospitalized at Lenox Hill for nearly a month, first to remove an internal hemorrhoid and later to remove her malfunctioning thyroid. Just before Christmas in 1952, she had suffered an unusually severe "spell" that lasted several hours. Over the next two months, she experienced an aching pain in her right hip that intensified and radiated through her leg as the day progressed. By evening, her entire leg had gone numb and she limped markedly. In February 1953, she returned to Lenox Hill, where she was diagnosed with a sciatica-type neuritis, nervousness, fatigue, and advanced arteriosclerotic heart disease.

This hospitalization at Mercy Hospital, which lasted nearly a month, was the most serious of all. Almost every night for the entire time of my mother's stay, as I closed my eyes to go to sleep I would see my mother falling from the stool, her body on the floor, the green fields of Ireland still flickering on the screen, Father O'Farrell administering last rites. "If we are going to die," my catechism explained, "God helps us die a holy death, but if it is better for us to get well, then He makes us better." I tried to understand the words "if it is better for us to get well." I couldn't imagine the conditions under which it wouldn't be better for my mother to get well, and I prayed harder than ever that God would agree with me.

While my mother was away, all the neighbors

helped out. Mrs. Friedle had lunch waiting for both Elaine and me when we came home from school; Mrs. Rust supplemented my father's meager skills in the kitchen by preparing casseroles and soups; and, as always, my sister Jeanne filled in everywhere. Every day, when my father returned from work, we went together to the hospital. I brought my homework as well as books to read to my mother. In this way, we tried to give the hospital room some semblance of our family life. But it was impossible to forget where we were. As I walked through the corridors, I averted my eyes from the metal beds where patients lay so still they seemed already dead. I turned away whenever an anxious-looking patient was being wheeled down the hallway into the operating room, and I held my breath to escape the ubiquitous smell of disinfectant. Everyone tried to put on the best face possible, but for the first time I could remember, my father, always so resolutely cheerful, could not conceal his fretfulness.

Some measure of distraction from the stark, white hospital room was provided by the crackle of the radio as we huddled around my mother's bed to share Dodger games. Fortunately, by September of '53, it was already clear that the Dodgers would win the pennant. It had been a brilliant season: "It's the greatest team I've ever managed," Chuck Dressen crowed. "It's a helluva outfit." Roy Campanella won his second Most Valuable

Player award with a batting average of .312, forty-one home runs, and a league-leading 142 runs batted in. Duke Snider led the team in homers with forty-two while hitting .336. Still possessed of a powerful will to win, the aging Robinson, playing mainly in left field, hit .329 with ninety-five RBIs. Gil Hodges, after a start so appalling that the Brooklyn clergy offered prayers for his revival, finished by hitting .302 with thirty-one home runs. Jim Gilliam, with his dazzling play at second, was named Rookie of the Year.

Sunday, September 6, was my father's birthday, which we celebrated in my mother's hospital room with cake and ice cream, listening to the Dodger game on the radio. It was a typical Dodger-Giant vendetta. In the second inning, Furillo (who had twenty-two hits in his last thirty-eight at bats, and would win the batting title that year) was hit on the wrist by a pitched ball. He picked himself off the ground, pushed two umpires and the Dodger manager out of his way, and headed toward the mound. Both dugouts emptied, and after a long interval, the game resumed. But no sooner had Furillo taken first than he turned and charged toward the Giant dugout, certain that Leo Durocher had ordered the pitcher to hit him. The pugnacious Durocher rose to meet him, and the two men converged, fists flailing. Teammates finally separated them, but in the melee a bone in Furillo's hand was broken, putting him out of action for the rest of the season. "I'll get him," Furillo fumed when he went to the hospital that night for X-rays. "On the field, on the street, or anywhere else I find him. I'm only sorry I didn't get a good sock at him. I wouldn't care if it cost me a thousand dollars and I wasn't worried about others ganging up on me because his own players hate him, too."

My mother was so infuriated by Furillo's injury that she suddenly sat up in bed and cursed Durocher in a voice more firm and spirited than I had heard from her for a long time. In a peculiar way, it became clear to me at that moment that she had turned the corner. In the days that followed, her condition began to improve, her appetite slowly returned, and she exhibited her old determination to recover her full strength.

A week later, the Dodgers clinched the pennant, earlier than any modern club, and met the Yankees in the World Series. Once again, Billy Martin was the Yankee hero, driving in eight runs on twelve hits. Even though everyone agreed the Dodgers had the better team, they lost yet again. But for the first time it didn't seem important at all. My mother was home from the hospital. Our family was together again. There would be other seasons, other chances.

IN THE SPRING OF 1954, when I came home for lunch, I often found that my mother had set up her ironing board in front of our television set to watch the Army-McCarthy hearings.

Indeed, all the mothers in the neighborhood were mesmerized by the dramatic confrontation between Senator Joe McCarthy of Wisconsin and the civilian chiefs of the Army. And what transfixed our mothers inevitably influenced us and, ultimately, would cast an ugly shadow over our own play.

In February 1950, with the country still stunned by the shock of the Soviet nuclear bomb and the invasion of South Korea, Joe McCarthy had burst onto the national scene when he told a Republican audience in Wheeling, West Virginia, that he had a list of 205 known communists in the State Department. Although no such list was ever produced nor any actual communist unearthed, the explosive speech opened one of the most destructive chapters in American political history. For more than four years, McCarthy's scattershot accusations of treason created an atmosphere of fear and anxiety that imperiled civil liberties, ruined reputations, disrupted careers, and destroyed countless lives. The entire panoply of congressional inquiries, executive investigations, accusations, and blacklists came to be known by the single word "McCarthyism."

In 1954, his reckless arrogance swollen by political success, McCarthy went after the United States Army. His starting point was the refusal of Major Irving Peress, an Army dentist, to answer questions about his alleged membership in the American Labor Party. Though Peress was no longer in the Army, he had been promoted to major before his discharge. "Who promoted Peress?" McCarthy demanded day after day, until the question became a refrain. He called for the Army's personnel files so he could determine who was involved in this "conspiracy" to promote and protect a "known communist." Army Secretary Robert Stevens refused McCarthy's demands until leaders of the Republican administration, fearing the issue was dividing and weakening the party, urged him to furnish the records. Stevens' seeming capitulation set off a storm of protest around the world. The London press said that McCarthy had accomplished what General Burgoyne and Cornwallis had never achieved—the surrender of the United States Army.

Stung by the criticism, Stevens fought back. He denied that he had surrendered, refused to give up the files, and insisted that he would never allow Army personnel to be browbeaten or humiliated by a congressional committee. The stage was set for a showdown. There followed an unprecedented trial by congressional committee on television, in which the Army responded to McCarthy's charges with accusations of its own, claiming that McCarthy and Roy Cohn, his chief investigator, had tried to extort favors from the Army on behalf of a former subcommittee consultant, David Schine, who had been drafted.

The hearing supplanted even the soap operas as our mothers went about their daily routine to the clangorous accompaniment of lawyers, senators, Army officers, and the coarse interruptions of Senator McCarthy. In the evenings, our fathers were filled in on the events of the day. And, not understanding what was at stake, we made a game of our own out of McCarthyism, a child's version of accusation, personal attack, and bitter dispute.

As the hearings progressed, even those somewhat sympathetic to McCarthy began to turn against the senator. A growing revulsion was fed, not simply by the absurdity of his attack on the patriotism of the U.S. Army, but through television's pitiless daily exposure of his coarsely abusive manner and his reckless disregard for facts. The inevitable end came in an exchange between McCarthy and Army counsel Joseph Welch, a patrician Boston lawyer. Angered and frustrated by Welch's persistent cross-examination of Roy Cohn, McCarthy charged that Welch had planned to bring a young communist from his Boston law firm to work with him on the hearings. When Welch disregarded the attack, McCarthy named the young man, Frederick Fisher, and charged that Fisher had been a member of the Lawyers Guild. In fact, after discussing Fisher's law-school membership in the Lawyers Guild, both Welch and Fisher had decided it would be best for the young man to stay behind. And now, for no compelling reason, out of the purest malice, McCarthy was trying to destroy him.

Stunned by the unexpected accusation and close to tears, Welch turned to McCarthy: "Until this moment, Senator, I think I never really gauged your cruelty or your recklessness. Have you no sense of decency, sir? If there is a God in heaven, this attack will do neither you nor your cause any good." When Welch finished his eloquent and emotional riposte, the crowded hearing room burst into applause. Reporters rushed to the counsel's table, where McCarthy sat alone, his head in his hands. "What did I do?" he asked, a look of bewilderment on his face. What he had done was to reveal himself to the entire nation as a savage and self-aggrandizing bully. The hearings continued for a few more days, but McCarthy was finished. His blistering attacks would no longer find a sympathetic audience in the nation at large.

Our children's version of McCarthyism would come to a similar end. We had begun by transforming our living rooms into a counterpart of the Senate chamber. We set up a table facing a single chair in the middle of the room. The person designated as the accused sat in the chair while the rest of us asked questions and made charges from behind the table. As our accused fidgeted uneasily on the stand, we grew increasingly hostile, interrupting explanations with points of order, claiming we had documents and proof to back up our accusations. We shouted and argued just as we had seen the counsel do on television. Day after day we played the treacherous game, even though one of us usually ended up running from the room in tears. We accused one another of being poor sports, of cheating at games. We exposed statements of the "accused" which denigrated others. Marilyn Greene accused Elaine of saying that the new girl on our block, Natalie, was fat; Elaine accused Marilyn of saying that Eileen was a crybaby. I accused Elaine of whining that Eileen always took the role of mother in our games of house. Eddie accused Eileen of complaining that Elaine was too bossy. Often these charges were true. We did, indeed, talk behind one another's backs, but we had never imagined that our slurring words, bad-mouthed comments, and hurtful language would be made known to others.

When I was on the stand, Eileen Rust charged me with pretending that she and I were best friends while Elaine was away on vacation. She claimed that, within minutes after Elaine had departed for Crescent Lake, Maine, in the Friedles' packed Hudson, with their bird in a covered cage on the back seat, I had raced over to Eileen's house and told her that she was my best friend. For two weeks, she said, we had played together every day. But as soon as Elaine returned, I had lost interest in her. What Eileen said was true. "I didn't mean to hurt you," I cried, as I burst into tears.

As the games progressed, they became even more vicious and mean-spirited. Marilyn said she knew the truth about my family, that my real mother had died when I was born, that my mother was really my grandmother. Stung by the attack, I lashed back: "How can you say such a thing? Your name isn't even Greene. It's Greenberg. You're the one who's hiding things, not me!"

Our game created rifts between us, dividing us into rival camps, until we finally grew tired, and a little afraid, of the anxiety and the nastiness. One day, as we sat in our circle trying to decide whose turn it was to be the accused, we chose instead not to play anymore. It was as if a terrible fever had gripped us, and now it was broken. We moved the chair and table back to their proper places and never again conducted our mock trials.

CHAPTER SIX

The arrival of adolescence altered my relationship to my family, diverted my attention from the Brooklyn Dodgers, and distanced me from my best friend, Elaine Friedle. My appearance, the thoughts that demanded my attention, the different ways I related to the pleasures of my childhood—everything was changing, and I was in control of neither the direction nor the nature of these changes. Now my daydreams, which had once been filled with the sight of Jackie Robinson leaping to snare a line drive, were occupied with thoughts of Howie Rabinowitz and Danny Schechter, the most handsome boys in my junior-high-school class. Most troubling to one who had always maintained a resolutely cheerful disposition, my moods shifted unpredictably. Some evenings, I happily sat with my parents and watched the Dodgers play. Other nights, I would suddenly find their company oppressive and would withdraw to my room to listen to Chuck Berry, Little Richard, and Fats Domino.

The complications of being a twelve-year-old were increased by my graduation from a small, familiar grammar school to the much larger South Side Junior High, whose pupils came from different parts of the town. Many kids from other grammar schools seemed more sophisticated and stylish than did my neighborhood friends. Two of the other grammar schools drew from areas far more affluent than ours. A third school was made up of mostly African Americans. Amid this initial confusion, we all scrambled to make new friends and find out where we belonged.

My separation from Elaine, who was one grade behind me and would not enter junior high for another year, made my adjustment more difficult. For as far back as I could remember, Elaine had been my best friend, the first person I called in the morning, the last person I spoke to at night. And even after we finished talking, we had continued to send messages across our driveway on our second-story clothesline-pulley. Elaine, full of energy, enthusiasm, and adventure, had planned our days, devised and organized our games, led our expeditions. Her fearless assertion of ideas and opinions commanded my respect. Now, for the first time, we had different schools and different circles of friends.

The distance created by our separate schools was lengthened by the changes of adolescence. The alterations in my body were gradual, and I remained thin and angular. My period came, but without the pain and headaches that Elaine experienced. She was now the tallest person in her class, and her large breasts seemed to encourage boys who had been her friends to jostle her and whisper teasing remarks. Formerly bold and outspoken, Elaine became withdrawn and bookish, slumping forward as she walked and rounding her shoulders protectively. Her confidence, particularly in relation to boys, began to diminish. She even began to worry that her passion for and extensive knowledge of baseball were a liability in a girl and would further alienate the boys.

Elaine's parents could not comprehend her unhappiness. Her older brother, Gary, was one of the most popular boys in the high school. In the spring of '55, he was nominated to run for president of his class. Every afternoon, Gary's fervent supporters gathered in the Freidles' basement to construct posters and placards for the campaign. "Don't tarry, vote for Gary," read one sign, with a sluggish turtle painted on the front. On the day Gary won, Elaine and I watched him ride down our block in an open car with his girlfriend June, followed by dozens of high-schoolers beeping their horns to celebrate his victory.

"Don't worry," Mr. and Mrs. Friedle assured

Elaine. "Boys will start calling once you learn how to handle them. Stop talking, start listening. Ask them what they like to do. What interests them, what are their hobbies? Focus on *them,* not yourself." The Friedles' recommendation reverberated throughout the fifties—the self-effacing woman was the ideal; in order to be attractive to others, popular magazines and books admonished, a girl had to conceal her intelligence, subordinate her own interests. To the extent she catered to the ego of others—i.e., men—a woman would find approval and acceptance.

"If only I'd been given permission to read my books, play my piano, and think about baseball, I might have been fine," Elaine said many years later. "But when the boys didn't call, my parents forced me to call them, to invite them to dances at our church. It was excruciating. I would call them up, I would ask them about their stupid hobbies, and still they would turn me down. Then, on Sundays, when our city relatives came to our house, they would ask scornfully, 'What's the matter? Can't you find anyone you like better than yourself?'"

I tried to talk Elaine out of her sadness. Sometimes I could make her laugh recalling the silly songs we used to sing on the way to the beach, recounting the terror of our trespass onto Old Mary's property, or remembering the thrill of disobedience when the matron at the Fantasy Theatre banished us for throwing the bag of popcorn over the balcony railing, but I couldn't console her about the present or the future. Her lack of social confidence gave way to depression, a barrier I could not penetrate. Although Elaine was one of the smartest and best-read girls in school, her extreme nervousness and self-consciousness made any public appearance difficult. She told me that once, in the middle of delivering an oral book report, she got so nervous she broke off in the middle and ran from the room.

Although I did my best to comfort her, my attention was directed to understanding and mastering the brave new world of junior high. I had become part of a new circle of friends. We were not the cheerleaders, the prettiest girls, the best dressed, or the daughters of the richest families. My friend Judy's father owned a television-repair store, Nancy's father was a lawyer, Valerie's parents ran the local bookstore. None of us could match Sheri Hoffman's glamour, her long thick ponytail, her slender waist emphasized by the thick cinch belt she always wore. Nor could we boast her fabulous wardrobe, with cashmere sweater sets in different shades of pastel, coordinated Papagallo flats, and perfect circle poodle skirts held aloft by three crinolines. My friends, however, were smart, popular, talented, and involved in a multitude of after-school activities. Marjorie wrote poems that were published in our local paper, Valerie was a talented science-and-math student, Judy was a stellar Ado Annie in our school production of *Oklahoma!*, Nancy was near the top of our class, and Susan was the only one of us who could make herself faint on demand. Except for me, everyone in our group was Jewish. Our circle was large enough that we never lacked a pal to sit with at lunch, hang out with on weekends, or call on the phone. Every Saturday in the late fall and winter, we went to the movies together, flirting with boys with ducktail haircuts and turned-up shirt collars. In threes or fours, we went ice-skating on Hickey Field, shopping at A & S in Hempstead, and bowling on Maple Avenue. We attended sock hops, pep rallies, football games, and basketball games. Invariably, we ended our evenings at the Pantry, our favorite diner. Crowded together in small upholstered booths, we sat for hours, talking, watching boys, and playing our favorite songs on the table-side jukebox.

My father never accepted the cultural conventions that crushed the ambition and imagination of so many girls. He did not agree that girls should subdue their competitive instincts, or alter their behavior to make themselves attractive to men. He urged me to run for class office, try out for the school plays, and speak up in class if I had something to contribute. When he learned I was going to see a cowboy movie I had already seen and disliked just to please a boy, he shook his head disapprovingly. "You wasted your time once," he said. "Don't do it twice." Elaine's feeling that her parents had invested their energy in promoting her brother Gary's aspirations while counseling her to conceal her own gifts and desires, was shared by many young girls whose brothers became the focus of their parents' ambitions. Perhaps my father's attitude was different because he had no sons, or perhaps it could be traced to his love for his sister, Marguerite, who had been his closest childhood companion.

The fact remained, however, that it was the men who took the trains and went off each morning to make money and pursue careers while every woman in my neighborhood, without exception, was occupied solely in managing a household and caring for children. It was my great and lasting good fortune to attend a school where the dominant voices on the teaching staff belonged to a group of women whose careers and lives provided eloquent opposition to the social conventions of the time. Several of these women had been made department heads during World War II, while the men were in the service. In contrast to Rosie the Riveter, however, they did not leave the world of work and responsibility when the men returned; instead, they devoted the rest of their lives to bringing about social, educational, and, in the end, political change. Since then I have had exceptional teachers at Colby College and Harvard University, but I can't remember a more original, vivid, and committed group of teachers than the half-dozen or so women I had at South Side Junior and Senior High.

Mrs. Nardino read us the poetry of Emily Dickinson and long passages from her favorite novel, Emily Bronteau's *Wuthering Heights,* until we, too, were captivated by the saturnine Heathcliff and the bleak beauty of the moors. "Who would you marry?" she challenged our class, "the gentle Edgar Linton, and be mistress of civilized Thrushcross Grange, or the elemental Heathcliff up on the Heights?" The boys in the class smirked and shrugged, but finally someone said what was in every girl's mind—Heathcliff. "Of course, Heathcliff," she said, laughing. "Everyone wants to be browbeaten by Heathcliff. Water your choice down and transport it to the Deep South and you'd prefer the scalawag Rhett Butler over the steady Ashley Wilkes, wouldn't you?"

I was already an old hand at enmeshing my own life with the lives of the characters in my books, and didn't think the choices were as stark as Mrs. Nardino made them seem. I, too, would have chosen to live at Wuthering Heights. But I would figure out a way not to be browbeaten by Heathcliff. I would soften the place and try to domesticate Heathcliff himself. But if I succeeded, I wondered, would I end up with an Edgar Linton? With her probing style, Mrs. Nardino forced us into the books we read, provoking us to debate issues of motivation, gender, and power, to analyze the nature of relationships.

Miss Sherman approached literature from a different perspective. Her chief interest lay in understanding the different societies and cultures depicted in the novels we read. She was partial to the novels of Willa Cather,

Thomas Hardy, and Nathaniel Hawthorne, in which the landscape and the nature of the society are decisive in determining the fate of the characters. She made us understand the grim moral judgment of Puritan New England and how it weighed on Hester Prynne, and gave us a feel of what it would be like to be young Àntonia on the Nebraska prairie in the days of the pioneer. At the end of the school year, she handed out exhaustive summer reading lists that she had carefully compiled with enticing synopses under each title. We would compete with one another to see who could finish the most books on the list.

Mrs. Brown had a passion for geography and seemed to possess an encyclopedic knowledge of every lake, mountain, and river in every country, together with the chief products that each country produced. Her maniacal intensity compelled us to memorize what seemed like the capital of every country on the globe. We were forced to commit to memory all the major stops of the Trans-Siberian Railway from Moscow to Vladivostok and beyond, to the port station of Nakhodka—with extra credit offered for those who could further delineate the stops on the Trans-Manchurian line, the Trans-Mongolian line, and the Baikula-Amur offshoot. Though her famous map tests inspired our fear, her engagement with her subject commanded our respect.

My favorite teacher, Miss Austin, taught "citizenship education," an amalgam of history and government, my introduction to how our democracy was formed and how it worked. She was a large and impressive woman, deeply committed to civil rights and social justice, who regularly decried our generation's lack of political commitment and implored us to know what was happening around us and to take an active part in political affairs. On at least two occasions I can remember, she wept openly in front of our class: the first when she read a speech by Adlai Stevenson calling for a renewal of national purpose, the second when she re-created President Roosevelt's death. At the time I was taken aback, unable yet to understand how political feelings were powerful enough to make one weep.

I tried to describe these remarkable women to Elaine, their commitment to their subjects and their skill in communicating their passion to us. I was certain that her confidence would be bolstered once she fell under their spell. I pictured myself taking her around the hallways, introducing her to my favorite teachers. I missed my best friend and I wanted her to believe in herself once more. "Just wait till you get here," I told her again and again. "You won't believe some of these teachers....The way they talk about books, history, the whole world. It's so exciting. You'll love it, I promise."

IRONICALLY, IT WAS the same passion for baseball which Elaine thought alienated boys that provided the surest foundation for our changing friendship. None of my new girlfriends cared about baseball the way we did; none could debate comparative lineups or pitching staffs like Elaine. She was the only one who had seen me jump for joy when the Dodgers won a close game or seen me cry when they lost the playoffs or the World Series. She was the only one who could tease me about Jackie Robinson as I could tease her about Billy Martin. When we talked about baseball, we were simultaneously talking about our shared friendship.

As the 1955 season got under way, there was a sense among Dodger fans that time was running out for Brooklyn. The extraordinary continuity of the lineup over the years had intensified our loyalty, but now the heart of the team was growing old. Because of advancing years and a variety of injuries to his legs, the thirty-six-year-old Jackie Robinson could no longer dance on the base paths with the agility he had shown in his early career. Pee Wee Reese was also showing signs of age. His throws from deep in the hole could no longer catch a fleet runner; he was no longer an All-Star shortstop. Gil Hodges was thirty-one; Campanella and Furillo were both thirty-three. Preacher Roe had retired. Campy was coming off surgery for a broken wrist that had reduced his batting average in '54 to a meager .207, and Furillo's average in '54 had dropped more than fifty points from his career performance in '53. If our team was ever to requite our love with the

World Series victory we had longed for, it had to be soon.

The Giants of Leo Durocher, on the other hand, had just won the 1954 World Series. "It's hard to explain what it feels like," Max told me many months after the Giants had beaten the formidable Cleveland Indians in four straight games. "I've had a happy winter, warming myself replaying those four Series games in my mind. When I close my eyes at night, I can still see that miracle back-to-the-plate catch Willie Mays made in the first game. Winning the world championship...it's like nothing you can imagine."

I didn't begrudge my friends in the butcher shop their satisfaction. It had been twenty-one years since the Giants had last won the World Series. Still, no matter how long the gap between victories, the fact remained that the Giants now boasted *five* world championships, whereas the Dodgers had never won a single World Series. Seven times we had won the pennant, and seven times we had lost the Series: the first to the Boston Red Sox in 1916, the second to the Cleveland Indians in 1920, and then five straight to the Yankees, in 1941, 1947, 1949, 1952, and 1953. No other team had come so close so many times without winning.

On opening day of 1955, the Dodgers, the eternal bridesmaids, stood along the third-base line in the Polo Grounds as the captain of the Giants, Alvin Dark, proudly raised two pennants up the pole at the top of the clubhouse—the 1954 National League flag, and the world championship banner, which had never flown over Brooklyn. "I looked over at the Giants," Jackie Robinson later said, "and thought of the kick they must be getting out of it. After all, you see people and you have to try to put yourself in their place sometimes. It was like Thomson's homer. Bad as we felt, after it was all over, you couldn't help feeling how thrilled he must be, and what a great thing it was in baseball. So today I just tried to realize how they were feeling at that moment."

If my interest in baseball had seemed dormant, it was awakened with a start when the Dodgers began the '55 season with ten victories in a row. When the Dodgers' first winning streak was stopped, they promptly forged a second one, this time winning eleven straight, twenty-two out of twenty-four, to give them a staggering nine-and-a-half-game lead over the Giants by the middle of May. During the streak, the Dodgers pulled every aspect of their game together: the hitting, the pitching, and the defense. Almost everyone in the starting lineup was hitting .300 or better, and the pitchers—Carl Erskine, Don Newcombe, Billy Loes, Russ Meyer, and Johnny Podres—combined for an ERA of only two earned runs per game.

While the Dodgers were tearing up the National League, Elaine was in a state of anxiety over the Yankees, locked in a four-way fight with Cleveland, Boston, and Chicago.

Casey Stengel had radically changed the team after its failure to win in '54, acquiring pitchers Bob Turley and Don Larsen from the Orioles to join Whitey Ford in the starting rotation, and adding Elston Howard, their first black player. Billy Martin, who had missed the entire '54 season, was still in the Army, however, and Elaine was certain the Yankees couldn't win without him.

Though Elaine's attraction to the shrill, wiry Martin remained inexplicable to me, in the name of our friendship I resolved not to mention his big nose, hot temper, or foul mouth. She kept Martin's picture by her bed, and searched the papers each day for news of his impending return. When he was finally released from the service at the end of August, she was the happiest I had seen her in months. For years afterward, even after Elaine got her Ph.D. in English, married, and had children, her father sent her an annual Valentine's card in the name of Billy Martin, bearing the inscription that always made Elaine laugh: "Aching for you, waiting for you, Billy."

EVEN THOUGH the Dodgers were flourishing, and school was more exciting than ever, new tensions had developed at home, due, in part, to my own petulance concerning the simplest household chores. Though I had once found pleasure in putting away the dishes with my father or helping my mother hang out the clothes, I now found myself resenting each chore I was asked to perform. Embarrassed that our lack of an electric dryer left my underwear hanging out on the line for all to see, I was even more distressed by the possibility I might actually be seen fixing a clothespin to my bra or to my mother's girdle. I rarely refused my mother's requests directly: I simply claimed I was busy with something important and would get to it later.

My resentments were displayed more openly when my parents kept me from going to movies I wanted to see. As Catholics, we were expected to be guided by the assessments of the National Legion of Decency, established to protect Catholics from immoral films. Since 1934, parishioners had been asked to take an annual pledge, asserting that "I condemn indecent and immoral motion pictures and those which glorify crime or criminals....I acknowledge my obligation to form a right conscience about pictures that are dangerous to my moral life. As a member of the Legion of Decency, I pledge myself to remain away from them." The Legion classified films in three categories—those suitable for adults only, such as *Marty* and *East of Eden;* those objectionable in part for all ages like *Sabrina, A Star Is Born,* and *Blackboard Jungle;* and those decisively and ominously labeled "Condemned," like *Game of Love* or *Garden of Eden.* There was a separate category for *Martin Luther,* deemed unacceptable because it offered a "sympathetic and approving" representation of the life and times of the Protestant leader. Seeing a film that the Legion had disapproved was not automatically a sin. But seeing a film that was immoral in the eyes of God was sinful. The purpose of the Legion was to help the faithful make the right judgment, and its proscriptions, though not decisive, were taken seriously in many Catholic households, including my own.

Despite the warning of the Legion of Decency, I did not see how there could be any harm in seeing *East of Eden*. Its recommendation didn't say the film was bad, only that I was too young. And every one of my girlfriends had seen it and enthused breathlessly about James Dean, who played Cal Trask, an angry young man vying for his father's approval. I had already read John Steinbeck's saga, retelling the biblical story of Cain and Abel through two generations of families in California's Salinas Valley, and I could see no reason why the movie should be off-limits. After much persuasion, my parents relented. Elaine and I went and were immediately enamored of the sulky young actor with his curled lip and troubled eyes. Every Monday, we haunted Brand's soda store in the hope that James Dean would be featured in *Photoplay* or *Modern Screen*, the glossy movie magazines that we now perused as eagerly as we had once sought the newest comic books.

I made less headway with my parents when it came to *Blackboard Jungle*, the story of an idealistic teacher in a slum-area high school, a film which introduced "Rock Around the Clock," the hit song by Bill Haley and the

Comets. The Legion of Decency objected to the film, the *Long Island Catholic* reported, because "it glorified crime, condoned immoral actions and contained suggestive dancing." The Legion found particularly disturbing a scene in which the teacher tries to introduce his students to classical jazz, only to have his precious record collection smashed to bits. "Even when the hero, (played by Glenn Ford), finally breaks through the animosity of his students, you are not encouraged by his prospects," the Legion advised. "Before that, the hoods are shown raising hell in classrooms and corridors. Hoodlums are glorified on screen in such a way as to promote delinquency."

When my parents refused to let me see the movie after I had badgered, cajoled, and pleaded, I blew up. I turned to my mother in a flash of anger and said, "You've always told me I should form my own opinions and not let other people do my thinking for me."

"It's not about opinions," my mother said. "It's about stupid, excessive violence."

"But how do you know?" I shouted. "How do you know it's offensive? You haven't even seen it."

Here my father intervened, informing me in a very low voice that he found my tone to my mother offensive. Furious, frustrated, I raced to my room, slammed my door, and turned up the volume on my radio as high as it would go. For hours, I sulked on my bed, hoping the sounds of Alan Freed's rock and roll music on WINS would filter down into the living room and disturb my mother's peace as she played the piano.

Every dollar I earned that summer was spent on 45s. "Shake, Rattle and Roll," "Sh-Boom," "See You Later, Alligator," "Blueberry Hill," "Chantilly Lace," the Everly Brothers, Little Richard, the Platters, and of course Elvis Presley. When Elaine and I weren't watching baseball, we retreated to her finished basement to listen to rock-and-roll records and practice dancing. Our parents had sent us to dancing school to learn the waltz, the fox-trot, and the two-step, but our formal lessons had taught us nothing about moving to the beat of rock and roll. Occasionally Mrs. Friedle would appear at the head of the stairs to tell us that our repulsive music was actually shaking the house, but normally we were allowed to practice without trespass so long as we stayed in the basement. More than ever, I wished that we had our own finished basement, a place where my friends and I could escape the watchful eye of my parents. Everything about my parents had become a source of humiliation, from my mother's dowdy aprons to my father's excessive pride in my accomplishments. I yearned for a room of my own larger than my tiny bedroom.

IF THERE WERE NOW occasional blowups, the general atmosphere in our household remained relatively undisturbed: we still played Scrabble every Sunday night, worked together on the *Times* crossword puzzle, and, most of all, shared the transcendent play of the Dodgers. By the middle of July, the Dodgers were more than thirty games above .500. Week after week, they continued to win, and the roar of the crowd emanating from our black-and-white television filled our house all that glorious summer.

At the end of the day on Friday, July 22, as I was preparing to go to the movies with my girlfriends, my father called me excitedly to tell me he had managed to get us tickets to the thirty-seventh-birthday celebration of Pee Wee Reese. "A consummate professional," he would always say when talking about Reese, "a gentleman who lives by a code, a work ethic that delivers the goods day in and day out." Even though I was mildly disappointed at the thought of missing a movie date with my friends, I didn't want to dampen his enthusiasm. When he suggested we go an hour or so early to see the pregame ceremony honoring Reese, I decided to take along my autograph book. As it turned out, I was glad I did.

Just before the celebration was to begin, I caught Jackie Robinson's attention as he headed slowly to the dugout. I didn't care that Robinson's hair was now almost totally gray. The aging warrior remained my favorite player. I had traded for Robinson's autograph with Eddie Rust, but I had never made direct contact with him myself, never looked him in the eye, and I wanted his name linked to me in a more intimate way.

I leaned over the railing, and with my most beseeching smile waved my autograph book, opened to a page with an empty space surrounded by a wreath of florid messages: "Let's never forget one another....Remember me until rubber tires and Niagara falls....May you have a succession of successive successes....I will always cherish our relationship." Before signing, Robinson scanned these silly, affectionate sentiments, and I could feel my face reddening. Then he wrote for a long moment. "Well," he said, "I can see I'm in good company." He closed the book, handed it back to me, and, with a laugh, descended into the dugout. I was settled beside my father and the special celebration had already begun before I dared to open the book. My heart beat faster until I felt almost dizzy, for there in the middle of my dearest friends' messages were the words:

Keep your smile a long, long while. Jackie Robinson.

I would not let the book out of my hand as I watched baseball executives and Reese's teammates gather for the ceremonies. As Reese approached home plate, I thought about the very special relationship which existed between Robinson and Reese—the black pioneer and the Southern captain. When Robinson first came to the Dodgers, it had been Reese who quashed the petition against him by his teammates. And on an overcast day in Cincinnati, with fans yelling racial epithets and hurling containers toward the grim-faced

Robinson, the respected Reese—team captain and Southern gentleman—called time, slowly strode across the infield, put his hand on Robinson's shoulder, and spoke to him softly, one man to another. The crowd was quieted, as were the members of the Cincinnati team, and the story soon spread through the world of baseball. It was a pivotal moment in Robinson's struggle, and, in retrospect, one of the finest moments in the history of baseball. Now, as Reese walked forward to receive the tributes of his peers and the loving acclaim of the crowd, Robinson reached out in a swift, barely noticeable gesture and put his hand on Reese's shoulder. "Reese and Robinson," my father remarked, "they're a lot more than great baseball players."

After tributes of mixed eloquence were spoken, birthday gifts were presented, including a new Chevrolet, three thousand dollars in war bonds, a television set, golf clubs, cameras, and fishing equipment. The master of ceremonies was Dodger announcer Vin Scully, who had replaced Red Barber the previous year. Scully guided the emotional Reese to the microphone. "When I came to Brooklyn in 1940, I was a scared kid," Reese began. "To tell you the truth, I'm twice as scared right now."

After the fifth inning, an enormous birthday cake was carried onto the field and the lights in the park were turned off. That was our signal to light the candles we'd been given when we arrived, and to join Gladys Gooding on the organ to sing "Happy Birthday." The thirty-three thousand candles flickered in the night like the Milky Way. Not only did the Man of the Hour double twice and score a run in the Dodgers' 8–4 victory, but the generous wit of Jackie Robinson had given me an unexpected moment I would treasure for the rest of my life.

That night with my father, Reese, and Robinson remained fixed in my mind as the Dodgers continued their extraordinary season. On September 8, 1955, they clinched the National League pennant earlier than any team since 1904. The game was their eighth straight victory, and they finished seventeen games ahead of the second-place Braves.

In the American League, the Yankees remained in a close struggle with the Indians, the White Sox, and the Red Sox. Throughout August and the early part of September, no team was able to build a lead of more than two games. While the race seesawed, Dodger fans debated which team they would rather play in the World Series. The debate was resolved when the Yankees, sparked by the return of Billy Martin, as Elaine had known they would be, won fifteen of their last nineteen games to clinch the pennant on September 23. So, once again, the two ancient adversaries prepared for the contest I most wanted and most feared.

ALTHOUGH OUR SCHOOL PRINCIPAL, Dr. Richard Byers, refused our request to pipe the first game over the PA system, we managed to follow the action at Yankee Stadium through portable radios, with notes passed from desk to desk, and by observing the reactions of classmates. When I saw a look of pain cross the face of my friend Moose Fastov, a devoted Yankee fan, I knew that something good must have happened. Paul Greenberg, who was listening via earphones to a radio surreptitiously tucked under his desk, had just signaled him that Jackie Robinson had tripled to left and scored on a single by Don Zimmer. The Dodgers were ahead 2–0. Barely ten minutes later, however, Moose's fist shot triumphantly into the air when Elston Howard's home run off Newcombe tied the score, 2–2. During the break between classes, Duke Snider homered off Whitey Ford to put the Dodgers up 3–2, but by the time French class had begun, the Yankees had tied it again. When the bell signaled the end of school, it was already the seventh inning and the Yankees led 6–3. Afraid of missing the decisive action if we dashed for home, we gathered on the outside steps of the school building to listen to the final innings. Liberated from the constraints of the classroom, I screamed when the ever-amazing Robinson stole home in the eighth. But in the end, the Yanks held on to win the game, 6–5.

Even though the Series had just begun, the voice of doubt now entered into confrontation with the voice of hope. "They've lost the first game." said doubt. "It looks bad. They're going to lose the Series again, just as they always have."

"It's only one game," countered hope, "and it was in Yankee Stadium. It was a close game, they played well. Tomorrow is another day."

But by the end of the following day, doubt, swollen by fear, was in the ascendancy. The Dodgers had lost again, by a score of 4–2, on a five-hitter by Tommy Byrne. Was the Series already gone? For the past thirty-four years, no team had ever come back to win a Series after being down two games to none. And Dodger history did not encourage dreams of a historic comeback. There's more to life than baseball, I told myself, with the wisdom my twelve years had given me. There was the Sadie Hawkins dance, for instance, and my choice of a date. And there was my paper on Reconstruction.

"Don't give up now," my father admonished me. "They'll be coming back to Brooklyn. Home-field advantage is a big thing, and nowhere is it bigger than at Ebbets Field." And he was right. The Dodgers roared to life in the third game, banging out eight runs and fourteen hits. Surprise starter Johnny Podres pitched a complete game to celebrate his twenty-third birthday; Campanella hit a home run, double, and single; and Jackie Robinson ignited the crowd and his teammates when he unnerved Yankee pitcher Bob Turley with his daring on the bases.

My pleasure over Robinson's virtuoso performance and the Dodgers' victory was cut short that night when Elaine called to me from her window. She was so overwrought I could barely understand her and feared that something catastrophic had happened in her house. "Just meet me outside," she said tearfully. I ran down the stairs and met her under the maple tree. She threw her arms around me and told me she had just heard on the radio that James Dean had been killed. His Porsche Spyder had careened off the road between Los Angeles and Salinas. His neck had been broken and he had died instantly.

For a long while we barely talked at all. Then we talked half the night. No one was awake in either of our houses, and soon all the lights on our block were out. There was no banter about that afternoon's game. We were two twelve-year-olds lying on our backs, surrounded by darkness, looking up at the autumn sky and talking fiercely about death and James Dean, who was not so much older than we were, grieving as perhaps only two teenage girls can grieve. Above us, the leaves of the maple tree rustled, and as we looked up at the night stars, the spirit of James Dean seemed very close.

I was exhausted the following day and watched drowsily as the Yankees jumped ahead with two quick runs off Carl Erskine. But when home runs by Campanella, Hodges, and Snider put the Dodgers ahead 7–3 in the fifth, my suddenly revived spirits dissolved all fatigue. In the next inning, the Yankees reduced the Dodger lead to 7–5, scoring two runs on a double by Billy Martin. But in the eighth, Campanella scored an insurance run and the Dodgers held on to win 8–5. The Series was now tied at two games apiece.

Overcoming the disaster of the first two games, the Dodgers had captured the momentum. They won the fifth game on Sunday afternoon as rookie Roger Craig and reliever Clem Labine held the Yankees to three runs while Brooklyn scored five times. "This could be both the day and the year," the *New York Post* predicted in a front-page story Monday morning. "This better be 'next year,'" one fan was quoted as saying. "If the Bums blow this one, the cops better close the Brooklyn Bridge. There'll be more people taking long dives than in 1929."

The sixth game began on Monday, while we sat in Mrs. Brown's geography class. The boys who had the portable radios with earphones sat against the back wall and sent messages forward as each inning progressed. We were studying Mongolia that day, and Mrs. Brown asked us to name Mongolia's three main products. "Yaks, yurts, and yogurt," my friend Marjorie answered. Suddenly there was a muffled roar from the back of the room. Bill Skowron had just hit a three-run homer, putting the Yankees ahead of the Dodgers 5–0. "Well, class," Mrs. Brown said, with a knowing smile, "I'm glad you find the three products of Mongolia as thrilling as I do." Then, to our amazement, she put a radio on the front desk and let us listen to the game. Unfortunately, the Dodgers never got started, and the Yankees won easily by a score of 5–1, tying the Series at three games apiece.

Before my father left for the Williamsburg Savings Bank the Tuesday morning of Game Seven, he promised to call as soon as the game was over. "I feel good about our chances today," he said, as he kissed me goodbye. "I've been waiting for a championship since I was a lot younger than you, and today it's going to happen at last."

"Do you really think so?"

"I really feel it." He winked at me and was off to work.

My morning classes stretched out endlessly before game time finally arrived. At noon, we were astonished to hear Principal Byers' voice telling us to report at one o'clock to our homerooms. We would be allowed to listen to the deciding game over the PA system.

When the lineups were announced, I was dismayed to learn that Jackie Robinson was not starting. Hobbled by a strained Achilles tendon, he was replaced by rookie Don Hoak. My only compensation was the not unwelcome news that an injury to Mickey Mantle would keep him from the Yankee lineup. Young Johnny Podres was on the mound, trying to post his second victory of the Series and win it all for the Dodgers; Tommy Byrne was pitching for the Yankees. In the early innings the classroom was tense, as neither team was able to score. Then, in the fourth, Campanella doubled, moved to third on a groundout, and reached home on a single by Hodges. The Dodgers were ahead, 1–0. In the sixth, they scored again on a sacrifice fly by Hodges.

Even though the Dodgers held a 2–0 lead, there were no sounds of celebration, no blustering talk from the Dodger fans in our class. We were a generation that had been nurtured on tales of tragedy, and memories of defeat: 1941, 1949, 1950, 1951, 1952, 1953. The prideful Yankee fans among us were composed, waiting for Berra or Martin or some other hero to overcome the Brooklyn chokers and transform looming defeat into victory. In the bottom of the sixth, it seemed that their time had come. Billy Martin walked on four straight pitches. Gil McDougald followed with a perfect bunt single. With two on and no outs, Berra came to the plate. Had I been home, this was the moment I would have fled the room, hopeful that when I returned Berra would be out. As it was, I had no choice but to remain at my desk, sandwiched between Michael Karp and Kenny Kemper, certain that trouble was brewing.

It was a little after three in the afternoon when Berra came to bat. The bell ending the school day had just rung, but we sat immobile in our seats, heard the portentous crack of the bat, and listened as the ball sailed toward the distant corner of left field. Some 150 feet away, left fielder Sandy Amoros, having shifted toward center anticipating that Yogi would pull the ball, turned and began his long chase. The Yankee runners, Martin and McDougald, rounded the bases, their faces turned toward the outfield, watching for the ball to drop for a certain double. But Sandy Amoros, fleet of foot, gallant of will, raced to within inches of the concrete left-field wall, stretched out his gloved hand, and snatched the ball from the air. For a moment he held his glove aloft, then, steadying himself with one hand against the wall, wheeled and rocketed the ball to Reese, the cutoff man, who, in turn, threw to first to double up McDougald.

We were going to win. At that moment, I knew we were going to win. Amoros' spectacular catch augured victory just as surely as Mickey Owen's dropped third strike in '41 had foretold defeat. The gods of baseball had spoken. I ran the mile to my home, anxious to see the end of the game with my mother in familiar surroundings. When I reached home, the score was still 2–0, and it was the bottom of the ninth. Give us three more outs, I prayed. Please, God, only three more outs. I sat cross-legged on the floor, my back leaning against my mother's knees as she sat on the edge of her chair. She edged forward as the first batter, Bill Skowron, hit a one-hopper to the mound. Two more outs. Bob Cerv followed with an easy fly to left. One more out. Elston Howard stepped to the plate. After the count reached two and two, Howard fouled off one fast ball after another, then sent a routine ground ball to Reese at shortstop, who threw to Hodges at first for the third and final out.

There was a moment of frozen silence. Then Vin Scully spoke the words I had waited most of my life to hear: "Ladies and gentlemen, the Brooklyn Dodgers are the champions of the world." Later, Scully was asked how he had remained so calm at such a dramatic moment. "Well, I wasn't," he said. "I could not have said another word without breaking down in tears." Just as Campanella leaped up on Podres, I jumped up and threw my arms around my mother. We danced around the porch, tears streaming down our cheeks, as we watched Campanella, Reese, Hodges, Robinson, and all the Dodgers converge on the mound, with thousands of delirious fans in pursuit.

After the final out of the seventh World Series game, which earned the Dodgers their first ever Series victory, pitcher Johnny Podres jumps high in the air as Campanella rushes toward the mound, literally walking on air. As we watched the Dodgers converge on the mound, my mother and I danced around the porch, tears streaming down our cheeks.

"We did it! What did I tell you, we did it!" my father bellowed merrily when he reached us minutes later. His call was one of tens of thousands made between 3:44 P.M. and 4:01 P.M., as parents, children, friends, and lovers exchanged screams, shouts, and expressions of joy. Trading on the New York Stock Exchange virtually came to a halt. On that afternoon, the phone company later estimated, it had put through the largest volume of calls since VJ day a decade earlier. "Listen," my father said, holding the phone to the open window of the Williamsburg Bank. "Do you hear the horns, the church bells, the factory whistles? It's absolute pandemonium. There's going to be one grand celebration here tonight. You two have got to come in. Take the next train and meet me at the bank as soon as you can."

My mother paused only to change her clothes, and the two of us were on the train heading for Brooklyn. We emerged from the subway into a crowd of hundreds, then thousands of people dancing in the streets to the music of a small band that had occupied the steps of the Williamsburg Bank. Bunting and banners flew from the windows, pinstriped effigies of Yankee players hung from the lampposts, confetti sifted down onto the sidewalks. The traffic was at a complete standstill, but no one seemed to mind. Finding his bus trapped at an intersection, a bus driver abandoned his vehicle and joined the revelers on the street.

My father suggested dinner at Junior's, a landmark delicatessen on Flatbush Avenue, just two long blocks north of the bank. The place was packed: eight or ten people crowded every booth. Some leaned against posts, many laughed, shouting and jumping ecstatically. We stood happily for an hour or more, hugging each new celebrant who walked in the door, until we finally found seats. In the booth next to ours, an old man boisterously announced that if he died the next morning he would go happily to his grave. We ordered corned-beef sandwiches, topped off by Junior's famous cheesecake.

Someone at Junior's said that the official celebration was taking place at the Bossert Hotel, where the Dodgers were scheduled to hold their victory dinner and dance that night. With scores of others, we took the subway to Brooklyn Heights and got off at Montague Street. There, standing behind police barricades, we joined tens of thousands of Dodger fans hoping to catch a glimpse of our heroes as they made their way into the old-fashioned hotel with its marble pillars and ornate ceilings. As the players walked in, they greeted the crowd. Even after their dinner began, they kept returning outside to wave to us again. Walt Alston posed with a group of teenagers while the crowd serenaded him with "For he's a jolly good fellow." A gray-haired woman in a wheelchair reached up to Johnny Podres and he bent down to kiss her. Even the reticent Carl Furillo was caught up in the exuberance of the night. "Oh, God, that was the thrill of all thrills," he later said. "I never in my life ever seen a town go so wild. I never seen people so goddamn happy." At last, Robinson appeared and spoke to the crowd. "The whole team knows it was the fans that made it for us," he told us. " It was your support that made this great day possible. We thank you from the bottom of our hearts."

No one wanted the night to end. When my father turned to ask my mother how she was holding up, she replied she felt twenty again. He led us to the foot of Montague Street, where a promenade overlooking the East

River offered a view of the Statue of Liberty and the lights of Manhattan. Ever since the day in 1898 when Brooklyn had given up its proud history and independent status to merge with New York City, Brooklynites had lived in the shadow of Manhattan. Each new slight—including the demise of the famed *Brooklyn Eagle* earlier that year—only reinforced the perception of second-class citizenship. But this night was Brooklyn's night. This night, Brooklyn, not Manhattan, was the center of the world.

Never again would Dodger fans have to wait till next year. The world championship was theirs. As the *Daily News* proclaimed in the next morning's banner headline: "This IS next year!"

CHAPTER SEVEN

During the next few years, as the world of my childhood began to slip away, I would often remember that magical evening. I would remember my mother as she stood at the edge of the river overlooking the city, the soft light from the street lamp smoothing the lines of her face. I would recall the laughter of my father, the merry vitality of the crowd, and the Dodger players who returned our adoration with a devotion of their own. My life had been held fast to a web of familiar places and familiar people—

my family, my block, my church, my team, my town, my country. They were part of the way I defined myself. I was not only Doris Helen Kearns, but a Catholic, a resident of Southard Avenue, a Dodger fan, a Rockville Centre girl. Everything was wonderfully in order. But things would soon change, and when they did, I, too, would be different.

For as long as I could remember, our family had been on intimate terms with every neighbor on our block. I knew the layout of our neighbors' houses as well as I knew my own. So familiar were the print sofas in Elaine's living room, the texture and smell of the stuffed chairs in the Lubars' sun porch, the thick rugs in the playroom at the Greenes', the round kitchen table at the Rusts', that I could have maneuvered my way in the dark through every house on our block.

The Goldschmidts were the first to move. As more families migrated to the suburbs each year, automobile sales continued to grow. Mr. Goldschmidt's Chevrolet dealership flourished, and the family built a new home in an affluent section of the neighboring town of Merrick. The Lubars were next to go. Beginning as a distributor of ladies' apparel at twenty dollars a week, Mr. Lubar had risen to become an executive vice-president at Robert Hall. His success made possible the purchase of a more spacious house in the adjoining town of Baldwin. Though they were sad to leave, the lure of more bedrooms and larger rooms proved irresistible. For Mr. Greene, the move was the "opportunity of a lifetime." Dow Chemical had developed a new property called "Styrofoam" which was reported to be superior to cork for insulation. When the company began awarding distributorships for promotion and marketing in various sections of the country, Mr. Greene applied for a position on the West Coast. Though he talked about how much he would miss the autumn leaves, the crisp winter air, the sleds on the snow-covered streets, he was excited when Dow granted him exclusive rights to sun-soaked southern California, a grant that eventually made him a very wealthy man.

The ties which had held our block together began to loosen. As each year passed, more of our weekday hours were absorbed by school activities. The street was no longer our common ground. Television, once a source of community, had become an isolating force. The corner stores continued to provide a common meeting place, but competition from two new supermarkets, Bohack's and A & P, would soon diminish traffic to the butcher shop and the delicatessen. The soda shop and the drugstore were no longer our hub of activity. The supermarkets would eventually be followed by two chain drugstores in the downtown area. In the years to come, one by one, the family-owned stores would disappear: the soda shop would be the first to go, then the butcher shop with Max and Joe, and finally the drugstore.

In the summer of 1956, when I was thirteen,

Elaine announced that her family was moving to Albany. Her father's bank, a small institution where he had been happily employed as vice-president in charge of commercial loans, merged with Bankers Trust. Though he retained his job, he lost the authority he had once enjoyed and increasingly felt decisions were being made behind his back. He grew so unhappy in his new situation that he began staying home. Elaine and I would return from school to find him sitting disconsolately on the stoop, withdrawn and silent. In June, Mr. Friedle had gathered his family together and told them he had accepted a new job in upstate New York. The move was set to take place at the end of the summer. Elaine's mother was grief-stricken at the thought of moving. The clapboard house, the garden, the tree-lined street, the corner stores were her world. Now she had to abandon the home she had created with loving care.

Elaine's impending departure suffused our friendship, lending an ominous, melodramatic, last-time quality to everything we did. At the very end of June, in celebration of Gary's graduation from high school, the Friedles put on a lavish party to which the entire neighborhood was invited, along with all their Jamaican relatives and Gary's friends. An elaborate buffet was laid out on the dining-room table. Towering piles of presents which Gary intended to open at the end of the evening stood on the kitchen table. The basement was set up for music and dancing. My parents stayed briefly, but the night was hot and the noise deafening, so they retreated to our porch, where they sat by the big electric fan and listened to the merriment next door.

While everyone was occupied upstairs, Elaine led her favorite uncle Roy to the basement so they could dance to the Four Freshmen's "Graduation Day." Roy had lost his wife, Elsie, to diabetes a few months earlier, and Elaine's mother feared he had sunk into depression. On this night, however, he seemed to be enjoying himself thoroughly, dancing Elaine around the floor. Suddenly he made what Elaine later described as terrible rasping sounds. At first she thought he was teasing and implored him to stop; then she realized that something was terribly wrong. He slumped to the floor and Elaine raced upstairs for help. Her father and several guests accompanied her back down to the basement, but by the time they reached him, Roy was already dead.

When the news spread to the party upstairs, Gary swept all his graduation presents off the table in one swift, violent gesture, and Dolly threw herself to the floor screaming. Soon relatives were shrieking and sobbing all around me. I ran home to tell my parents and stayed in my house while the police and ambulance arrived. Much later that night, Elaine called to me from her window. Her voice trembled. The romantic death of James Dean had not prepared either of us for Uncle Roy's death on the floor of her basement. On the occasion of Dean's death, we had talked half the night. Now all I could think of to say was, "I know, I know," trying to convince her and myself that I understood how she was feeling and that I felt it, too.

Roy's death sealed Elaine's unhappiness and brought an end to our hopes for enjoying our last summer together. I wanted her to share my grief over our imminent separation, but instead she looked forward to the move, comforted, she told me, by the idea that in a new place she would have "a chance to become another person." Her enthusiasm for departing made it difficult for me to tell her how terrible I felt. As the weeks went by, we were unable to talk about anything that mattered, and when the moving van finally arrived, it was almost a relief. I watched from my house as two burly men carried an endless stream of boxes, books, rolled rugs, and furniture out of the house. When the truck was loaded, we said goodbye in an odd, remote, dreamlike way. The Friedles got into their car and drove away. Four decades would pass before I saw Elaine again.

A new family moved into the Friedles' house next door, but I have absolutely no memory of them or of any of the children they might have had. Nor do I remember the people who moved into the Greenes' house across the street. As people left and time passed, I could still look out at the same houses, skirted by their tiny, neat, green lawns with the same flowering shrubs. It all looked the same. But it had all changed.

Images of the days when our block was an extended family rose in my imagination: the Sunday barbecues, our excited gatherings in the early days of television, reading with Elaine under the maple tree, and the marathon games of hide-and-seek. Summer had always been my favorite season. Now I couldn't wait for the opening of high school.

ALTHOUGH THE DODGERS won the pennant in 1956, it was an uneasy and disquieting season. Uncertainty about the team's future beclouded the summer days, diminishing pleasure in the season at hand. The previous August, in the midst of Brooklyn's triumphant ride to the World Series, Dodger owner Walter O'Malley had sent shock waves through the city with his announcement that the National League had granted permission for the Dodgers to play seven or eight "home" games in Jersey City, New Jersey. The announcement was considered a first step in O'Malley's campaign to find a new stadium for the Dodgers. Each year, despite one successful season after another, attendance at Ebbets Field had continued to slide.

Critics complained that Ebbets Field was too old and too cramped, situated in a neighborhood that was rapidly deteriorating as more and more middle-class families moved to the suburbs, leaving behind poorer blacks and Puerto Ricans. It was said that the new suburbanites were finding it more comfortable to watch the game on television than to venture into the city at night, and that no ballpark could survive with space for only seven hundred cars. I hated to hear talk about the deficiencies of Ebbets Field. I loved the old ballpark and couldn't imagine the Dodgers in any other place.

In the middle of May, 1956, I awoke to the stunning announcement that our nemesis, the feared and hated Sal Maglie, had been acquired by the Dodgers. Who could have imagined that the scowling Number 35, whose brush-back curve year after year had sent Dodger batters sprawling, would end up in a Dodger uniform? "I've no grudge if he has some mileage left in his arm," said my father, chuckling. "Well, I won't root for him," my mother said. "How many times has he tried to bean poor Furillo, Robinson, and Campanella?" Columnist Jimmy Cannon spoke for many Dodger fans when he wrote that life would hold no more surprises for him now that Maglie was coming to Brooklyn. It was as if "the Daughters of the Confederacy are building a monument to General Grant in Richmond."

Before the season was done, respect for Maglie's contributions silenced much of the initial opposition to the trade. He helped the Dodgers win the '56 pennant and performed yeoman duty in the World Series, which the Yankees won 4–3. He went the distance for the win in Game One and gave up only two runs and five hits in Game Five, where he had the misfortune to come up against Yankee pitcher Don Larsen's perfect game. I was grateful for the victories, but I could never bring myself to think of Maglie as one of us. Every time I saw Campanella walk out to the mound with his arm on Maglie's shoulder, I shuddered, unable to erase the image of Campy crumpled at home plate after one of Maglie's bean balls.

The idea of Maglie as a Dodger was bad enough; the concept of Jackie Robinson as a Giant was unthinkable. Yet, on December 13, 1956, Brooklyn announced that Jackie Robinson had been traded to the Giants for pitcher Dick Littlefield, a journeyman whose continual moves from one team to another presaged the modern era. Robinson, seemingly stunned, asked the Giants for a few days to think things over. "After you've reached your peak," Robinson said, "there's no sentiment in baseball. You start slipping and pretty soon, they're moving you around like a used car. You have no control over what happens to you."

News of the trade left me feeling saddened and empty. Jackie Robinson had entered the majors two years before I had learned how to score. His career had been my childhood. Without him I would never have cared for the Dodgers in the same way. I was not surprised when Robinson announced he would retire a Dodger rather than report to the Giants. I knew he would never wear a Giant uniform.

The loss of Robinson seemed to accelerate the talk of moving, as if the central mast of the big top was gone, and it was time to strike the entire tent and move on. The architect Buckminster Fuller produced a design for a bizarre domed ballpark. O'Malley floated a plan to construct a new stadium on a large parcel of slum land at the junction of Atlantic and Flatbush avenues. It was an ideal location, eliminating the need for parking since it stood at the terminus of the Long Island Railroad and the meeting place for two subway lines. But the controversial plan required the support of city officials to condemn the slum, compensate property owners, and sell the land to O'Malley, something no one in a position of authority was willing to do. In the meantime, Robert Moses developed his own plan for a multipurpose stadium in Flushing, Long Island, that would accommodate thousands of cars.

In retrospect, it can now be seen that baseball was changing. After fifty years of stability, during which fans could depend on seeing the same teams in the same cities, three major-league franchises, one after another, picked up and moved elsewhere, abandoning their fans in the hopes of securing increased revenues. The Braves of Boston were the first to go, moving in 1953 to Milwaukee. The following year, the St. Louis Browns became the Baltimore Orioles, and the year after that the Athletics of Philadelphia became the Kansas City Athletics. Though each owner was able to justify his move on economic grounds, the transactions signaled the ever-increasing intrusions of business considerations into the national pastime.

In 1957, the auguries of Brooklyn's betrayal

began to multiply. For the first time we heard that O'Malley might actually leave New York for Los Angeles. We learned that Baseball Commissioner Warren Giles had told O'Malley that he could not move to California unless another team went with him in order to make the long trip to the West Coast more economical for the rest of the league. O'Malley, it was reported, had begun talking with Horace Stoneham, owner of the Giants, about moving his team to San Francisco. Every day, a new piece was added to the dismal puzzle.

That summer, I joined thousands of fans signing petitions imploring O'Malley, city officials, and anyone who might help to keep the Dodgers in Brooklyn. I attended a clamorous "Keep the Dodgers" rally in the city. And I wrote a long, personal letter to O'Malley, begging him to consider what the move would do to the community and all the fans. On more than one occasion, I daydreamed of going to O'Malley's office to make the case for Brooklyn. I pictured a brown velvet couch in the middle of the room with its back to the drapes, two leather chairs encircling a small table, the floor covered with a large patterned rug. O'Malley was seated behind a cluttered desk, his thick eyebrows casting a diabolical shadow on his florid face. I was wearing my favorite dress, a black-and-brown-striped sheath, with black stockings and black high heels that gave me an extra three inches in height. He did not rise when I entered, but as I started to talk, his face softened, and when

I finished my monologue, a perfect blend of logic and emotion, he threw his arms around me and promised to stay at Ebbets Field. I had saved the Dodgers for Brooklyn!

It was, of course, only a fantasy. No flow of petitions, no appeal to loyalty or tradition could stop O'Malley once it became clear that Los Angeles was prepared to give him three hundred acres of prime land and five million city dollars to create new roads and improve access to the site. On August 19, 1957, Horace Stoneham announced that the Giants were moving to San Francisco at the end of the 1957 season. "We're sorry to disappoint the kids of New York," Stoneham said, "but we didn't see many of their parents out there at the Polo Grounds in recent years." Attendance at the Polo Grounds had been falling steadily each year. Indeed, without the eleven home games against the Dodgers, which accounted for nearly one-third of the box-office receipts for the entire year, the Giants could not possibly survive. The two teams were inextricably linked. On the day Stoneham made it official that the Giants were leaving, we knew that the Dodgers were also gone.

THE DODGERS played their last game at Ebbets Field on Tuesday night, September 24, 1957. Though everybody knew the Dodgers were playing there for the last time, the Dodger management had deliberately refrained from staging an official farewell. Consequently, fewer than seven thousand fans showed up, lending an even more forlorn quality to the evening. Duke Snider later recalled that it seemed as if the lights weren't working correctly, as if the game were played in twilight.

Pee Wee Reese led his teammates onto the field for the last time. Though the Dodgers won 2–0, there was no pleasure in the victory. We were in third place, ten games behind the pennant-winning Milwaukee Braves. The organist, Gladys Gooding, tried to honor the occasion with her own defiant ceremony, providing a medley of nostalgic tunes. After the Dodgers scored their first run, she played "Are You Blue," and "After You're Gone." The second run was accompanied by "Don't Ask Me Why I'm Leaving." As the game reached the final innings, she played "Thanks for the Memories," "When the Blue of the Night Meets the Gold of the Day," and "Que Sera Sera." After the last out was recorded, she started playing "May the Good Lord Bless and Keep You." Yet even this small gesture toward the feelings of the fans was interrupted when some Dodger official turned on the record always played at the end of Dodger games, "Follow the Dodgers." Nevertheless, Miss Gooding had the last say. For nineteen years her organ music had accompanied the Dodgers and she was determined to close out the program in her own way. As the opening notes of "Auld Lang Syne" drifted across the field, fans stood in clusters, arms around one another, many openly crying. Then, slowly, one by one or in small groups, the last fans left the stadium. Behind them, Ebbets Field closed its doors forever.

The following Sunday, the Giants held a special ceremony for their last game at the Polo Grounds, which at least provided a graceful opportunity for farewell. All the old Giant greats were on hand, and the crowd stood and cheered as Russ Hodges introduced each one: Rube Marquand, who had set a record in 1912 with nineteen straight victories, Carl Hubbell, Billy Jurges, Monte Irvin, Sal Maglie. The cheers continued as the starting lineup was announced: Whitey Lockman, Bobby Thomson, Willie Mays, Dusty Rhodes, Don Mueller. The last fan to leave was Mrs. John McGraw, widow of the celebrated Giant manager whose Giants had captured ten pennants earlier in the century. "I still can't believe I'll never see the Polo Grounds again," she said. "New York can never be the same to me."

The Dodgers officially announced their move a few days later in a terse statement that took no account of our feelings. Even the Yankees had the courtesy to issue a statement of regret that New York was losing the Dodgers and the Giants. In the hearts of Brooklyn fans, O'Malley had secured his place in a line of infamy which now crossed the centuries from Judas Iscariot to Benedict Arnold to Walter F. O'Malley. Effigies of the Dodger owner were burned on the streets of Brooklyn. It was all over. Never again would the streets of New York be filled with passionate arguments about which of the city's three teams had the best center fielder, the best shortstop, the best catcher.

In the butcher shop, we held our own farewell ceremony. Max put two pegs on the door that led into the giant freezer. On one peg he hung the black Giant cap I had given him in 1951; on the other I hung my blue Dodger hat. "Well," he said sadly, holding out his hand, "it's been something, Ragmop." We started to shake hands, and then clumsily broke off, so we could give each other a hug. "It sure has been something," I answered.

THAT SAME SEPTEMBER, my mother's health took a decided turn for the worse. The pain in her back and legs intensified, making it hard for her to sleep at night. Her eyes sank into dark hollows, and her already pallid cheeks took on a bluish tone. More than ever before, the slightest exertion left her exhausted. She complained of difficulty breathing until finally the doctors recommended hospitalization. The previous spring she had been hospitalized for two weeks; this time she would remain at Lenox Hill for nearly a month.

While she was in the hospital she suffered a stroke. Late one afternoon, she woke from a nap without sensation in her right foot and leg, and so dizzy she feared falling out of bed. Speech required great effort, and her words were slurred and difficult to understand. The doctors told us she had experienced a thrombotic stroke in the left side of her brain, causing partial paralysis on her right side. Apparently a blood clot had formed in one of her diseased arteries, blocking the flow of blood to the brain. Only time would tell if the damage was permanent.

Though the doctors assured us that most stroke survivors recovered fully and eventually regained use of their paralyzed limbs through physical therapy, I wondered if she had the energy or the will to recover. There was a frightened look in her eyes, and her weight had dropped to eighty-eight pounds, giving her tall frame an emaciated appearance. The war with her body over the previous decade had taken a terrible toll.

Slowly, however, she began to fight her way back. She gained some motion in her arm and then in her leg. A week after the stroke, she was up in a wheelchair; a week after that, leaning on an attendant's arm, she walked slowly down the hospital corridor, slightly dragging her leg. Her slurred speech had still not improved, but the doctors said she could go home if a hospital bed was set up on the first floor so she wouldn't have to climb stairs.

The bed was delivered and arranged in our living room a few hours before my mother came home. We had to roll up the rug and push all the furniture against the walls to make space for it. When my mother returned and saw the disarray caused by the giant bed, her eyes closed with weary disgust. The treasured order of her home had been disrupted, and she announced that she would practice going up and down the steps every day until "that thing, that intruder," as she called it, could be removed from her living room. Four weeks after arriving home, she had learned to negotiate the stairs, and the bed was carried away.

To celebrate the removal of the hospital bed, my father decided they should go out to dinner. She wore her favorite blue dress, the one my dad had so admired the night of the Red and Blue banquet six years earlier. I sat in their room, helping her get ready, uttering cheerful banalities, and, at the same time, wondering how she felt as she looked in the mirror and saw the partially paralyzed cheek, the deepened lines, the wrinkled skin that hung down from her upper arms. Then my father walked into the room and told her she looked wonderful. She responded with a smile so bright it seemed to me that she might believe him, that, in the reflected gaze of his steady admiration, she saw the face of the girl he had fallen in love with.

My mother's speech proved the most frustrating part of her rehabilitation. Though she never lost the ability to comprehend language, she had trouble finding the words she wanted, and her diction was indistinct. When the doctors suggested that it would be useful for her to read aloud, my father turned to me. Since my mother had come home from the hospital, I had stayed in school on many afternoons and spent an inordinate amount of time at the homes of my friends. I just wanted to escape, to pretend that nothing had changed. My fear of her illness had estranged us. Yet I could not witness my mother's ferocious effort to climb the stairs or prepare a meal without feeling ashamed. Now there was something I could do to help. I went to the library for an old friend we both loved—Dickens' *David Copperfield.*

"It's been a long time since we've taken turns reading to one another," I prodded her. She resisted at first, but once we got started, it became part of a routine we looked forward to each day. I remember her halting manner, reading the scene where Copperfield's aunt bursts out of the house because David Copperfield is a boy and not the "Betsey" she had confidently awaited. My mother paused when the scene was done, and suddenly we both started laughing. As the days and weeks passed, her voice and control grew stronger until, by way of Peggotty, Mr. Micawber, treacherous Steerforth, and loathsome Uriah Heep, all traces of a slur were gone from her speech.

Reading books together had once been a very significant part of my relationship with my mother. Now reading *David Copperfield* gave impetus to her rehabilitation, entertained us, dissipated my anxieties, and drew us closer than we had been in many, many months.

AS MUCH as I loved Dickens, however, there was nothing in his vivid portrayals of nineteenth-century London to prepare my mind for the disturbing events of mid-century America. As I stood in school to recite the Pledge of Allegiance or rose with the crowd at the ball park when "The Star-Spangled Banner" was played, it had never occurred to me to question, or even to think about, the words of the ritual I was reciting. I only knew that I was an American. And to be an American was a wonderful thing. I was aware, of course, that mistakes could be made, injustices committed. I had absorbed at least that much through my contacts with McCarthyism. But that could no more lead me to question the country itself than the acts of a renegade priest would cause me to question my Catholic faith.

The beginnings of doubt came through events which took place more than eleven hundred miles away. On the morning of September 4, 1957, armed troops of the Arkansas National Guard took up positions in front of Central High School in Little Rock. Governor Orville Faubus had ordered them to prevent the enrollment of nine black schoolchildren whose registration had been ordered by a federal court, pursuant to the landmark decision of the Supreme Court which declared school segregation unconstitutional. Since Faubus had made his intentions known in advance, reporters from television stations and newspapers across the country were there to witness the confrontation. Eight of the

243

nine children arrived together, accompanied by a group of black and white ministers. Through a failure of communications, the ninth child, Elizabeth Eckford, proceeded on her own.

Many hundreds of people shouted abuse as the small band of eight children moved toward the entrance. The Arkansas Guards, claiming they were acting under the orders of Governor Faubus, raised their bayonets to block the children's entrance. "What are your orders?" one of the ministers asked. "To keep the niggers out," a soldier responded. Unable to make their way through the phalanx of soldiers, the eight children and the ministers were forced to retreat.

When fifteen-year-old Elizabeth Eckford reached the school a few minutes later, she was greeted by a wall of hate. At the sight of the young girl standing alone, the irate mob descended on her, *The New York Times* reported, "baying at her heels like a pack of hounds." "Lynch her, lynch her," someone yelled. Finding the entrance blocked, Elizabeth turned around and headed back through the mob. With great difficulty, she finally reached the bus stop, where she collapsed on the bench, trembling, tears streaming down her cheeks.

Among the witnesses was a *New York Times* reporter, Benjamin Fine. We all knew Mr. Fine. He lived in Rockville Centre, and his daughter, Jill, was one of my classmates. He understood that as a reporter he was professionally bound to act as an observer, not a participant. But at the sight of the young girl, who reminded him, he would later say, of his own daughter, he entered the scene he had been sent to observe. He approached the tearful Elizabeth, put his arm around her, and lifted her chin, saying, "Don't let them see you cry." The menacing crowd of some five hundred closed around them, hurling threats and epithets. "Get a rope and drag her over to this tree," someone hollered. Suddenly a sympathetic white-haired woman fought free of the crowd and, with Fine's help, boarded the bus with Elizabeth to escape the melee. The crowd, frustrated and frenzied, then turned on Fine. "Now it's your turn," they shouted. "Grab him and kick him in the balls." "You got a nigger wife?" Mr. Fine did not answer. "Are you a Jew?" someone asked. "Yes," Mr. Fine said. "A dirty New York Jew? Have you been to Moscow lately?" As National Guardsmen stood by, the mob beat Fine badly enough to send him to the hospital. That night, Faubus made it clear he would continue to defy federal-court orders. Resolution ultimately would be in the hands of the president.

At the beginning of the school year, with the crisis in Little Rock looming, we were fortunate to have two teachers who thought much more could be learned from the drama in Arkansas than from the prescribed textbooks. Mr. Geise, our social-studies teacher, was a passionate liberal who, in his first year of teaching at South Side, had been an outspoken critic of Joe McCarthy. An anonymous note had arrived in his mailbox warning him that he wouldn't get tenure if he continued to make political statements. He threw the note away and continued to speak out. During Little Rock, *The New York Times* became our chief text, and each day we began our class with Ben Fine's dispatches.

"What's going on here?" Mr. Geise asked, opening our class discussion. "Can we, for a moment, put aside our emotions and see what forces are behind this conflict? Does a governor have the right to defy the order of a federal court? Who is the ultimate sovereign in a democracy? Where is the president of the United States in all this?" The questions Mr. Geise posed initiated a discussion that gave real-life content to the abstract concepts of federalism, sovereignty, and states' rights.

The news we debated and interpreted in social studies was enriched and amplified in English class by Mr. Jenkins, the first black high-school teacher hired to teach in Long Island. A graduate of Columbia College, with a master's degree from Teachers College, Mr. Jenkins had rapidly become one of the most respected and accessible teachers in the school. Day after day in classroom discussions, he combined humor with knowledge of history and literature to challenge our unconscious biases and dare us to think independently. When he heard us congratulating Jill on her father's bravery, he intervened. Of course Mr. Fine was brave, he said, but how would you

246

feel if a reporter had joined the angry crowd to help block Elizabeth from entering the school? Think with your mind, not just with your heart. Was there a line that had to be respected between reporting on an event and taking part in it?

That night, I sat with my parents as we watched on television the very events we had been discussing in school. We saw the mob surging forward to intimidate the young girl, the Guardsmen standing idly by, refusing to help her; the girl enduring the vulgarity with all the dignity she could muster. "Why doesn't Eisenhower send in federal troops to protect that girl? She's got every right to be there," I said, angrily echoing the arguments I had heard in school. "Why did you vote for Eisenhower anyway?" I asked my father.

"It's certainly an ugly, complicated mess," said my father, and then he began to smile. "I haven't seen you so upset since Bobby Thomson." "Well," my mother interrupted, "I know one thing, somebody should be doing something to protect that little girl." They were both right. Aside from the death of James Dean and the struggle to keep the Dodgers in Brooklyn, no public event had so fully engaged my private emotions. To challenge the president of the country, to berate angrily a governor I had never heard of from a place I did not know, was for me an immense expansion of political consciousness. It was a turning point, or, at least, the start of a turning point.

During the next two weeks, while the "Little Rock Nine" stayed at home waiting for the president to act, our teachers staged a mock debate for our class: "Should the president send in federal troops to desegregate Central High?" Mr. Geise played the role of Governor Faubus, passionately declaiming the impossibility of legislating emotions and feeling. "You cannot change people's hearts merely by law," he said, quoting President Eisenhower. Mr. Jenkins became a spokesman for the White House, arguing that federal troops would only provoke further violence, leading to a shutdown of all public schools in Arkansas and, perhaps, in other parts of the South. The position of the children and the NAACP was argued by two other teachers, who repeated the powerful reasoning of the Supreme Court that separate schools were inherently unequal and represented a denial of the constitutional right to equal protection of the laws.

When the debate was finished, we were asked to make a decision. It didn't take very long. Influenced by the grim reality of the images we had seen on television, we voted overwhelmingly to send in federal troops. I decided to draft a letter to President Eisenhower urging him to take the action we had recommended. I spent hours laboring over the composition of the letter. It was important to be respectful, to set forth arguments like those we had heard from our teachers—calm and reasoned, not an outpouring of anger. I proudly showed my effort to my parents and my teachers. If this doesn't persuade the president, I thought to myself, nothing will. The crisis dragged on for days, until Eisenhower finally decided to send in the troops.

The night of September 25, 1957, we watched exultantly as a long line of trucks, cars, and jeeps wound its way through Little Rock, while the state Guards, now under federal authority, joined with troops from the 101st Airborne Division to ensure the successful entry of the nine black students. "Oh, look at them," said Minnijean Brown, one of the Little Rock Nine. "It gives you goose pimples to look at them! For the first time in my life, I feel like an American citizen."

My classmates and I, children of the fifties, were entering upon a change in attitude, not wholly unlike that of Mr. Fine when he left his reporter's post to help a young black girl at Little Rock's Central High. Not satisfied to be observers of injustice, we undertook to right it. In a few years another decade would begin, one very different from the relatively calm span of my childhood. And we would all be part of it. The schoolchildren of the fifties would become the young men and women of the sixties.

LATER THAT YEAR we invited Ben Fine to address a special school assembly, expecting to hear a firsthand account of the action at Little Rock. We got more than we had anticipated. After briefly recounting his experiences, Fine instructed: "Don't think racial problems are just Southern problems. We in the North have very serious racial problems of our own."

He was right, of course. There was undoubtedly a large aspect of self-righteousness in our attitude toward race. We told ourselves that the mob of angry bigots we had seen on television had no counterpart in the North. Our own school system in Rockville Centre had been integrated for decades. Mr. Jenkins was adored by students at South Side, and each year we were certain to include a member of the black community in our student government. Even in music class, a progressive teacher, long before the era of "political correctness," had removed racist intimations from the old Stephen Foster songs we sang in class—supplanting the word "darkies" with "sweetheart" in "Old Folks at Home," and with "children" in "My Old Kentucky Home."

Mr. Fine punctured our complacency. A kindly, distinguished man with a gentle voice, he explained that housing patterns in New York City had produced a "de facto" segregation in schools that was every bit as damaging to young blacks as the formal segregation in the South. Even in our own village of Rockville Centre, he pointed out, anyone who cared could see that something had to be done about the blighted area known as the "west end," where the small black community of not quite a thousand people lived in badly substandard housing. Situated north of the retail district in an area three blocks wide and five or six blocks long, the west end had remained largely invisible to the rest of the town. Elaine and I had never ventured into the west end on our frequent bike trips, not because we thought it unsafe, but because it was not on our way.

Many of the houses, Fine told us, had primitive toilets, dangerous coal stoves, no central heating, collapsing stairs and walls. At least ten people were living together in one two-bedroom cold-water flat where the kitchen sink provided the only place to wash. In another old house, the mother slept in the dining room; two sisters, a brother, and an aunt slept in one bedroom; and a married sister, her husband, an aunt, a niece, and a nephew in the other. To be sure, there were a few well-kept homes within the dilapidated area. But the majority of the buildings were owned by absentee landlords who refused to make badly needed repairs and were satisfied simply to collect the monthly rents.

Not long after Fine's talk, Rockville Centre would commit itself to a controversial urban-renewal project. Convinced they were acting in the best interests of both the village and the residents, authorities approved a plan to raze the entire area and replace existing houses with a low-rise apartment building. The plan became the focus of a bitter battle as property owners with sound structures fought in vain to keep their houses. Even residents who hoped for improved living conditions feared the loss of the social structure provided by the old neighborhood. Initially, some black residents and activists, our teacher Mr. Jenkins among them, were active supporters of the plan; others charged that urban renewal was merely a device to eradicate the black section of the town. Year after year, through charges and countercharges, sit-ins and petitions, the project dragged on. More than ten years would pass before the plan was realized with the completion of a two-story brick complex known as Old Mill Court. In the interim, many of the black residents left the village and never returned.

The issues of race which had fired and enlarged my schoolgirl's mind had come home to Rockville Centre. They would soon become the focus of mounting dispute, of government programs and citizen protest, engulfing the North as well as the South in bitter controversy. In years to come, the afflictions of racism would lead me to the civil-rights movement, to political action far more involved than writing a letter to the president. I was still a patriotic American. But thanks to teachers of uncommon skill and breadth, patriotism would never again mean unthinking adherence to things as they were. I would not confuse the temporary leaders of a country with the country itself.

IF EVENTS in Little Rock stirred me to a new awareness of my relationship to the nation and its ills, another event, which also signaled the end of the decade, had no comparable impact.

I was at my boyfriend's house when the television news reported that the Soviet Union had launched Sputnik, a "space" satellite. Weighing nearly two hundred pounds and circling the earth every hour and thirty-five minutes, it was humanity's first successful venture into the fabled territory of outer space. "Listen now for the sound which forevermore separates the old from the new," the radio announcer intoned, alerting us to the pinging sound emitted by the satellite as it soared over the surface of the globe. Although I tried to listen, I couldn't hear the ping at all, but accepted on faith the repeated observation that the sound represented a serious defeat for the United States. Newspapers reported that Sputnik had given the Soviet Union a triple victory: militarily, it meant that Russia was far ahead of the United States in rocketry; politically, it gave the Russians an enormous jump in their efforts to be treated as a first-class power; and psychologically, it offered evidence that socialism was the wave of the future.

Since various sightings of the satellite were being reported in different parts of the world, my boyfriend suggested taking a blanket and binoculars to the park in the hope of seeing Sputnik as it whirled above the East Coast. As the dark set in, the trees seemed to close in around, and we strained our eyes to catch a glimpse of the artificial moon. We had been told that Sputnik was as bright as a star of the fourth magnitude, the dimmest star in the handle of the Big Dipper. Whether it was visible that October night or not I will never know, for, as we lay on our blanket, my boyfriend reached over and kissed me. It was not the first time I had been kissed, but always before it had been in a darkened movie theater or in the back of a car. On this clear autumn night, the spangled heavens seemed nothing more than a setting for romance. I didn't give Sputnik another thought.

MY MOTHER DIED sometime during the predawn hours of Saturday, February 22, 1958. On Saturday morning, while I was reading in bed, the phone in my parents' room rang, awakening my father, who yelled for me to take the call on the extension downstairs. It was my friend Valerie. I raced downstairs, made plans to go to the movies with Valerie later that day, and started back up to my room.

Halfway up the stairs, I heard my father calling for Jeanne, home for the holiday weekend. "Jeanne! Jeanne!" he cried. "My pal is gone....My pal is gone." I ran to my parents' bedroom. My father was sitting on the edge of my mother's bed, sobbing into his hands. My sister sat on the opposite bed, tears streaming down her cheeks.

"Mother is dead," my sister said. I reached for the bedpost to steady myself. Perhaps my mother's long illness, the dread sight of the hospital rooms, the visible signs of her deterioration should have prepared me for the prospect of her death. Yet the gap between a possibility—a word—and this reality was far too large for my imagination to bridge. I recoiled in shock at the sight of her body. "Are you sure?" I pleaded. "Did you listen to her heart? Call a doctor! Are you sure, Jeanne, are you really sure?"

"Yes," Jeanne said. "I'm sure."

My mother lay perfectly still on her back. She showed no evidence of pain, but her open eyes gave her face a startled look. "I saw her just after midnight," Jeanne said. "When I came in from my date, she heard me. We sat up talking while I had a cigarette. So it must have happened in the middle of the night.

"She never knew she was dying," my sister continued. "I'm certain of that. Look, her comforter is still in place." I understood immediately. Usually, mother's restless struggle for a comfortable position would throw her comforter to the floor by the time she woke in the morning.

As Jeanne spoke, my father stared fixedly downward. He didn't even look at me. His silence was unbearable. I put my arms around him and hugged him. I wanted desperately to comfort him and to find comfort for myself, but there was a terrible blankness to his eyes. I could see that he was having trouble breathing, as if shock had constricted his chest. "My pal is gone," he kept repeating. "My pal is gone."

Our family physician, Dr. Ben, arrived shortly afterward. He told us that either a massive heart attack or a massive stroke had caused her death. She was barely fifty-one. After Dr. Ben left, my father became increasingly passive. Jeanne made the necessary calls and decisions. Arrangements were made for Charlotte and Paul to fly home the following day, and the undertaker came for my mother's body. The rest of the day has vanished from my memory, except for the sight of our black cocker spaniel, Frosty, howling at the bottom of the stairs. Since he was injured as a puppy, Frosty had been unable to climb stairs. He loved my mother most of all, and each morning he would wait at the bottom of the stairs until she came down. On the day of my mother's death, and for weeks afterward, he remained at his post, waiting in vain for my mother's descent.

The next morning, I woke at my usual hour of seven o'clock. In the first seconds, as I rolled onto my back to stretch, there was no recollection of what had happened, and then every detail of the previous day flooded my mind—my first glimpse of my mother lying in bed, the startled expression fixed on her immobile face, the utter vacancy of my father's eyes, the grotesque intrusion of the men from the funeral parlor carrying the blanketed form down the stairs. No one was up yet. I wandered listlessly from room to room. I wanted my father, yet for the first time in my life I was afraid to disturb him. I wanted to call my friends, but did not want to be pitied. I wanted it all to go away, but knew it wouldn't. The phrase "I am fifteen years old and my mother is dead" sounded repeatedly in my head. I went downstairs and looked at our family album, turning to the photograph I had loved which showed my mother in her early twenties, her legs hung over the arm of the chair. I felt bitter. It did not seem fair, so much pain and sickness in a life so short. It wasn't fair to her. It wasn't fair to my father. It wasn't fair to me. Then I was ashamed. How could I think of myself now? It had been so much worse for her. Yet she had never complained. And now she was dead.

At the start of the three-day wake, I had to force myself to look into my mother's coffin. I avoided looking at her whole face, focusing instead on details—her gently waved hair, the odd color of the rouge which had been put on her cheeks. My eyes were drawn to the set of rosary beads strung around her long fingers, and then the wedding band on her left hand. In over thirty-one years of marriage she had never removed her wedding band from her finger. As a child, I had thought that the permanence of the marriage magically resided in that ring, and I would worry that something terrible might happen should the ring ever accidentally slip from her finger. Now there was no need to worry; the ring would accompany my mother to her grave. I reached over and touched her hand, but the thick cold of it filled my eyes with tears and my knees trembled.

Never had St. Agnes seemed so cavernous

as on the late-February day of my mother's funeral Mass. Although the cathedral could hold twelve hundred people, only the front pews were filled. But it did not seem empty. Everyone was there, all the people whose lives my mother had touched—the neighbors who made up the circle of her daily life, the men and women who ran the local stores at which she shopped, the milkman and breadman who came weekly to her door. And others, of course—my father's colleagues, my sisters' friends, and my own friends.

I could not concentrate on the Mass. I had no doubt that my mother deserved to go to heaven, but I couldn't picture what heaven was like. My childhood imagination had been stirred by the thought of an eternal dwelling place where all the members of my family would join with angels and archangels and live among the saints. I had taken some comfort in the teachings of my catechism that "at the end of the world the bodies of all men would rise from the earth and be united again to their souls, nevermore to be separated." It had all seemed so simple and so beautiful. But now I was puzzled; my knowledge seemed inadequate. Did the teaching of the catechism mean that my mother would live in heaven until Judgment Day with the body that had failed her on earth? Did it mean that on Judgment Day her body would be made whole and healthy, and if so, how could it still be her body? I sat in our pew, confused, each question giving rise to another. Think for yourself, my schoolteachers had told me. The Sisters had instructed us that there were answers, that faith would provide them. I tried to think. But I couldn't find answers. I would have to pray, I told myself. But for the very first time in my life, I wasn't completely sure that my prayer would bring an end to doubt.

I sat through the service with my jaw clenched. Occasionally I glanced toward my father, but he looked straight ahead, rigid, as if in a trance. After the burial, we returned home. I smelled the sweet pungency of the dozens of flower arrangements sent in condolence and I became violently sick to my stomach. Ever since, clusters of cut flowers have repelled me.

OVER THE NEXT FEW MONTHS, it seemed as if my life were being led by two different people. My activities with playmates on the block and my friends in school had always been a source of pleasure which helped obscure illness at home. Now I threw myself into high-school affairs with unprecedented zeal. I had many girlfriends, a steady boyfriend, and teachers I admired. I became an honors student, an officer of the student government, and, ultimately, would captain the victorious Red Team in the Red and Blue Meet. I had always found content for my fantasies in books. The works I now studied—the stories of great events and the people who shaped them— were not fantastical, but I found that I could shape them with my own understanding, make them part of my own experience in the way I had with the romance of Rhett Butler and Scarlett O'Hara. I came to treasure the small details that made an event or a figure from the distant past come alive. I fell in love with history.

At home, however, I entered into a private realm of sadness. The old rituals of family were gone, dissolved by death and my father's continuing grief. Though I dimly remembered a few occasions when my mother had reprimanded my father for "unwinding" too much on his way home from the train station, drinking now became a serious problem. During the days, my father remained sharp and clearheaded; he never missed an hour of work. But with increasing frequency, he returned home in the evening with the smell of whiskey on his breath. He staggered into the house, bumping into the piano, missing the step of the stair. His eyes, normally bright green, were bloodshot, his cheeks puffy. Increasingly, he drank at home, alone in the dark. Sometimes I tried to sit with him, hoping if I were there he wouldn't feel the need for drink. But, invariably, I'd end up talking on the phone, studying at a friend's house, or listening to music in my room. When I tried to talk with him about his drinking, I could not reach him. He insisted there was no problem for me to worry about. I began to feel that I had lost both my parents.

Without my sister Jeanne, who moved home after the funeral and commuted daily to Lenox

Hill Hospital, the months following my mother's death would have been unbearable. In some respects, my mother's death was even harder for Jeanne than for me: she had lost a confidante, friend, and counselor. Yet she willingly assumed responsibility for our home and for the needs of my father, allowing me to remain a teenager, free to focus on my activities at school.

Others have reported that after the death of a family member their home seemed larger, having become hollow, empty, and strange. My own house, on the contrary, seemed to shrink around us, the very rooms disappearing, as my father found himself unable to endure the porch where he and my mother had shared cocktails every evening, unwilling to eat in the breakfast nook where their day had begun, incapable of sleeping in the room where she had died. My father's depression left him no choice but to sell our house and move to a new place as quickly as possible. A buyer was found in May, and we planned to move to a garden apartment near the center of town in early July.

Although I understood my father's decision, I was sad, even resentful, at the prospect of leaving the only home I had ever known. The associations which compelled my father to leave only bound me more desperately to my home. For as long as I could remember, my sense of place, my past, and my identity had been rooted in this house, this street, this neighborhood. Almost every memory I had of my mother was connected in some way or other to the house, to the rooms where she had been virtually housebound. I could picture her standing at the back door talking to the bakery man, reading in her favorite chair on the porch, ironing in front of the television, or cooking at the stove. I was afraid that when we moved these images would be left behind, that I would forget my mother.

Reluctantly, I began to sort through my belongings. Since I had never liked to throw things away, I was fortunate that we had a big attic, accessible by a pull-down ladder, where I could store my valued possessions. Over the years, I had filled dozens of boxes with old report cards, books, baseball cards, programs, toys, dolls, board games, and letters from friends. Occasionally I would spend a few hours rummaging through my boxes. I liked the musty smell of the attic and the feel of the unplaned floorboards. Most of all, I liked to rediscover some old letter, or program, or scorebook to take me backward in time.

But I did not look forward to this trip to the attic. I would have to discard all but the few keepsakes that would accompany me to our small apartment. I sat in the middle of the attic floor, boxes piled around me. Wishing to postpone my painful task, I looked around the room. In one corner, an old baby carriage rested against the slanted window, casting a shadow on the floor. Across the room, two rocking chairs with broken slats stood side by side, along with some rolled rugs, a pile of

National Geographic, Saturday Evening Post, and *Life* magazines, and yellowing stacks of newspapers. Behind the newspapers there was an old wooden trunk belonging to my parents. I had never looked inside, but now I lifted the lid and uncovered a thick manila folder marked "Family Documents." I pulled out a sheaf of birth and death certificates arranged in chronological order.

I was thrilled with my discovery. Here, written in hand at the time of each birth and each passing, was the documentary history of my family, including the details which allowed me to picture the lives which had led to my own. The notice of my father's birth in 1901 revealed that his father, Thomas Kearns, was thirty-one and his mother, Ellen, twenty-eight, at the time of the birth, and that they had come to America from Ireland when they were twenty-one and eighteen respectively.

From this meager sheaf of brittle notarized documents whose handwritten words were beginning to fade, I began to create images of the past: the confident walk of my grandfather as he boarded the boat for America; his marriage to Ellen Higgins, whose family he had known in Ireland, the wedding ceremony in Brooklyn. I imagined my grandmother lying in bed, smiling, holding her first-born son, my father, Michael Francis Kearns. Although I had known some of the facts before, the official papers made the story come to life.

I kept reading. The death certificate of my father's brother, Thomas Jr., who had died at fifteen months, was stamped by the Brooklyn Department of Health indicating a communicable disease. The back of my neck shivered as I read the date and the time of the little boy's death, 5 A.M. on January 4, 1905—thirty-eight years to the hour before my birth! Next came the death certificate for five-year-old John, who had been hospitalized for nearly a month before he died from the wound in his leg. This was followed by the death certificate for my thirty-seven-year-old grandmother, Ellen. How strange, I thought, as I scanned the document, that she, too, like little Thomas, died at 5 A.M. And how very young they all had been.

The next document was titled "Death Certificate Number 799," verifying my grandfather's death at age forty. Uncomprehending, I read the stunning, unanticipated words: "Cause of death, Pistol shot to the head." And then, in the coroner's precise script, "Thomas Kearns. 633 Myrtle Avenue. Suicide." For my entire childhood, I had imagined the romantic tale of my grandfather, so sunk in grief over the death of his wife and child that he had died of a broken heart. No one had ever told me this, of course. But from the few facts I had been told, I had created a story which had become fixed in memory. Now I wanted to deny this new, far crueler reality. But there it was. In black and white. Undeniable.

My poor brave father, I thought. He had been such a little boy when it happened. What a powerful determination he had. Left an orphan, he had made a life for himself and for his sister, Marguerite. And then, even after her grim death in a dentist's chair had left him completely alone, he refused to yield, went on to make a future for himself and then for his family—for all of us. If I grieved for the loss of my mother, what must it mean to him, whose whole life had been drowned in death? My self-pity, my trivial resentments at the disruptions to my own life, drained away. I would be strong. I would help him. I loved him so very much.

Absorbed in my thoughts, I never even heard the footsteps on the ladder. I started at the sound of my father's voice.

"I see you found the family papers." His voice sounded small and weary. I looked guiltily toward the offending document in my lap.

"Why did you never say anything about your father?" I asked. "I thought he died of sadness."

My father didn't reply right away. He put his hand on my head and sat down beside me.

"I'm sorry," he said finally. "Sometimes you have to forget what you've lost and deal with what you've got."

I put my arms around him. I wanted to cry. I knew I shouldn't. "You see," he continued, "in a way you were right all the time. He did die of sadness. I would have told you about all this"—he gestured at the papers—"when you were older, when I thought it wouldn't hurt you or make you feel ashamed of our family." He sighed and surveyed my boxes. "My, you've really got a collection here."

"I wish I could keep it all." My eyes rested on a box of papers and mementos. "I know we won't have room for it, but I hate to throw anything away."

"You know," my father looked at me, "after my little brother died, then my parents, then my sister, one after the other, I used to wonder if things would ever be all right." He swept a layer of dust from the cover of an old Dodger scorebook that lay among the stack of cards, autographs, programs, and newspaper articles I had collected. "I know this move won't be easy on you, but I don't see any other way. I loved your mother so much. I still see her in every room."

"That's exactly why I wanted to stay." I stroked a blue felt pennant and tried to hold back tears.

My father squeezed my shoulders. "I'm sorry. It's strange the way something that comforts one person is so painful for another. Time will cure a lot of ills, but I don't think there's enough time in the world for me to get used to living here without her."

"It's okay," I said. "I don't care where we live. I just want us to be happy again."

"Do you still have every year?" my father asked, looking at the pile of Dodger scorebooks.

"Since 1949, when you gave me the first one."

"They were so close, so many times," my dad said, shaking his head. "Remember we said, if they just kept fighting, they'd make it in the end. And they did. We'll just have to do the same."

Then, for the first time in months, I saw my father smile. He pointed toward a discarded calendar which had been printed by a Brooklyn company after Bobby Thomson had destroyed the Dodgers' hopes. "Look at that," he said. And there it was, in large black type, Wait Till Next Year—the simple anthem that had served to comfort disconsolate Dodger fans and would now serve our family.

EPILOGUE

In March, 1965, seven years after the conversation in the attic of my house in Rockville Centre which closes this book, I flew to New York for my father's wedding. A few months earlier, my father had called me at my Harvard graduate school dormitory to tell me he intended to marry Florence Millea, an attractive outgoing widow who had been his companion of recent years. His voice on the telephone was hesitant, tentative, as if anticipating disapproval, but there was no equivocation, no concealed doubt in my enthusiastic response. My glad acceptance of his decision was fueled by a feeling of pride at the way he had overcome the crippling impact of his grief, the latest and most profound tragedy of a life marked by death and loss. In the years after my mother died, I had watched as he tapped the strengthening springs of his native resilience, stopped his drinking, and began to travel through America and Europe in the company of Mrs. Millea— visiting the distant cities and mountain villages which my mother had known only through books. As we talked, he interrupted my enthusiastic monologue: "She makes me happy, Bubbles." And I almost cried.

At the entrance to the pale granite Our Lady Chapel at the rear of St. Patrick's Cathedral, my sister Jeanne embraced me. In the years after my mother's death, Jeanne had taken on the responsibility of tending the family and me, and was now at Catholic University studying for her master's degree in science and nursing. Jeanne would go on to a distinguished career as an executive director of a regional nursing organization in the state of Colorado. Charlotte's responsibilities to her two young daughters and her husband, Paul, a thoracic surgeon at St. Jude's Hospital, had kept her at home in Fullerton, California, where she still lives, still beautiful, and still active in her own community of family and friends.

I watched the wedding ceremony with mingled feelings. It was a hopeful new beginning for my father; and for me, it was a final liberation from lingering concern and guilt. But it also, at least symbolically, marked a dissolution of my ties to the world of my girlhood, transporting the immediacy of experience into the world of memory where it would forever remain.

Although time and events outdistanced and reconciled my personal losses, my anger over O'Malley's treason still persisted. At Colby College and in my first year at Harvard—where I would teach for almost a decade before leaving to become a full-time historian—I refused to follow baseball, skipping over the sports pages with their accounts of alien teams called the Los Angeles Dodgers and the San Francisco Giants. Then, in my second year of studying for my doctorate, a young man invited me to Fenway Park. Allowing my desire for his companionship to overcome my principled reluctance, we took the subway to Kenmore Square in Boston, and together we walked up Lansdowne Street to the park. There it was again: the entrance up the darkened ramp disclosing an expanse of amazing green, the fervent crowd contained in a stadium scaled to human dimensions, the players so close it almost seemed that you could touch them, the eccentric features of an old ballpark constructed to fit the contours of the allotted space. I watched the players, the dirt scars which marked the base paths, the knowledgeable fans shouting their imprecations and exhortations.

For years I had managed to stay away. I had formed the firmest of resolutions. I had given myself irrefutable reasons, expressed the most passionate of rejections. But I could not get away. Addiction or obsession, love or need, I was born a baseball fan and a baseball fan I was fated to remain.

Nor could I have found a team more reminiscent of the Brooklyn Dodgers than my new team, the Boston Red Sox. Perpetual bridesmaids, exciters of hope and destroyers of dreams, the Red Sox often made Boston seem like Flatbush North. Mickey Owen's dropped third strike and Bobby Thomson's home run would be matched in baseball legend by Bucky Dent's pop-fly home run which lost the division and Bill Buckner's error which lost the World Series. Now, once again, every season would begin with large expectations and end with large disappointments, a scenario beautifully adapted to the somewhat masochistic temperament shared by Brooklynites and Bostonians alike.

Nor could anyone else in my family escape our shared past. Charlotte, obviously possessing a maturity and capacity for detachment far larger than my own, roots for a team called the Dodgers somewhere west of the Appalachians. Jeanne would become an acolyte of the Colorado Rockies, an expansion club just beginning to create its own history and traditions.

My father, like so many disinherited New Yorkers, turned to the New York Mets, and we resumed our baseball dialogue. When the Red Sox lost the seventh game of the World Series in 1967, my father was quick to instruct that I must not let the defeat destroy the memories of a glorious season. And during the final weeks of the Mets' amazing drive to the world championship in 1969, we would discuss the day's events almost every evening. It almost seemed as if, through the medium of baseball, we could recreate the old intensities—the loving, counseling father and his adoring, curious daughter—which had helped form my girlhood.

Shortly after my father died in 1972, the fatal heart attack coming as he watched a Mets game on television, I married and began to raise a family of my own, finding myself reenacting many of the rituals I had shared with my father. I took my oldest son, Richard, to spring training, and watched with an almost jealous pride as the generous Jim Rice let him feed balls into the pitching machine while the All-Star slugger took batting practice. I taught my two youngest sons, Michael and Joe, how to keep score, bought season tickets, and took them to dozens of games every year.

Sometimes, sitting in the park with my boys, I imagine myself back at Ebbets Field, a young girl once more in the presence of my father, watching the players of my youth on the grassy fields below—Jackie Robinson, Duke Snider, Roy Campanella, Gil Hodges. There is magic in these moments, for when I open my eyes and see my sons in the place where my father once sat, I feel an invisible bond among our three generations, an anchor of loyalty and love linking my sons to the grandfather whose face they have never seen but whose person they have come to know through this most timeless of sports.

When the 1986 Red Sox went to the World Series against the Mets my boys were certain the Sox would win. That certainty was a gift of youth that I could no longer share. Cruel experience had taught me that no expectation of triumph was unsullied by the possibility of defeat. Still, in the tenth inning of the sixth game, with the Red Sox ahead and only one out away from victory, I overcame my caution. My husband and I brought out the victory champagne. But even before we could open the bottle, an easy grounder went through the first baseman's legs, the game was lost, and the hopes of a world championship were smashed. As I sat in front of the television set in tears after the Sox lost the final game, my two youngest boys rushed to console me. "Don't worry, Mom, they'll win next season."

That's right," I said, forcing a smile, "there's always another season." I did not remind them that the Red Sox had not won a World Series for seventy years. There would be time enough for them to learn a harsher truth, I thought. But not yet. Not till they're older. Then, as they continued their concerned assurances, I realized that my mature wisdom was a deception. They were right. They were absolutely right. There would be another season. There would be another chance.

WYNCOOP WALK at Coors Field in Denver contains a quadrant labeled "1995 Coors Field Inaugural Season." In that quadrant can be found Brick Number 1334 purchased by my sisters and me. On the brick is graven "In memory of Michael Francis Aloysius Kearns." From that spot, on a summer night, one can hear the cheers of Rockies fans, and the occasional satisfying crack of a bat as it propels a ball toward the Colorado sky.

ACKNOWLEDGMENTS

The most valuable source material for this memoir was a series of interviews with my sisters, childhood playmates, school friends, and teachers. Though we moved from Southard Avenue more than forty years ago, I was able to track down almost every person who lived on my block. Most of these people I hadn't seen or talked to in more than three decades. Finding them again was the most satisfying part of writing this book.

Elaine Friedle and I had lost touch with one another several years after she moved to Albany. When I started my research two years ago I found her living in Germany, where she teaches English literature. After we exchanged more than a half-dozen long letters, we made arrangements to see each other at her brother's house in Connecticut. It was an extraordinary evening, not only because Elaine has a photographic memory for our childhood, but because once we started talking, the years began to fall away. I could see once more the face of the young girl who had been my best friend, I could hear the familiar voice that had reached my bedroom window so many nights before we both fell asleep.

I found Eileen Rust living in New York City, where she runs an art gallery; Elaine Lubar Moskow married with children on the West Coast; Rose and Sid Lubar in Baldwin, New York; the Barthas and Joe Schmitt's widow, Anna Mae, in Florida; Julia Rust and Max Kropf's wife, Melitta, in Long Island; and the Greenes in California. Each of my old friends and neighbors had a particular store of recollections that remained uppermost in their minds. As we talked, we sparked each other's memories; half-forgotten details slowly began to emerge.

In addition to my childhood playmates, I interviewed about a dozen school friends and teachers who generously shared with me their own recollections, along with diaries, letters, yearbooks, pictures and reading lists. I am grateful to Robert Geise, Ken Jenkins, Susan Gilman Krieger, Judy Lehman Ruderman, Valerie Ger Ostrower, Jill and Lillian Fine, Howard Rabinowitz, Robert Fastov, Marjorie Rosen, Marsha Gillespie, and Marjorie Garber.

My thanks also to the staff at South Side High School, especially Dorothy Zaiser, who was always available to help with her time and knowledge of South Side and Rockville Centre history; the staff at the Rockville Centre Public Library, including Rhoda Friedland, Ruth Levien, and Gretchen Browne; the staff at the Nassau County Museum, the Long Island Studies Institute, Dr. Barbara Kelly and Dr. Mildred De Riggi; the Schimmenti family; Diane Hackett, owner of the present Bryn Mawr Delicatessen; and Eugene Murray, mayor of Rockville Centre. For information on St. Agnes and recollections of growing up Catholic, I am grateful to Reverend Monsignor Robert Mulligan, Rector, St. Agnes (deceased); the Sisters of St. Dominic, Amityville, New York; Elissa Metz; Marilyn O'Brien; Margaret Williams; Pam Shannon; Nancy Dowd; and Grace Skrypczap. I thank Mary Stuart, who played Joanne Barron on *Search for Tomorrow* and shared her experiences as a pioneer in early television. For information on the urban renewal project, I owe thanks to Barbara and Jim Bernstein, Toni Ehrlein, Rockville Centre Historical Society, Doris Moore, and Reverend Morgan Days. For sharing remembrances of the Dodgers, I thank Neil Krieger and Barry Moskow. For general research on the fifties, I turned to my longtime research assistant, Linda Vandegrift. For the original idea of writing a memoir about my years as a Brooklyn Dodger fan, I thank Wendy Wolf.

At Simon & Schuster, where I feel I have found a warm and welcoming home, I owe thanks to my publisher, Carolyn Reidy, whose enthusiastic response to the book spurred me on when I wasn't at all sure I was going to finish on time; to Liz Stein, who once again shepherded the book through its various stages with good cheer and consummate skill; to Lydia Buechler and Terry Zaroff, who copyedited the manuscript with flawless skill; to my publicists Victoria Meyer and Kerri Kennedy; to Wendell Minor, who painted the elegant cover; and, of course, to my longtime editor and good friend, Alice Mayhew, whose continual support, confidence, good judgment, and editing prowess proved critical once again. It is now more than twenty years that we have worked together and I look forward to twenty more. This is my first book with Binky Urban as my literary agent, and what an absolute pleasure it has been to have her at my side in a relationship I deeply treasure.

For additional readings of the manuscript, I thank Clark Booth, James Shokoff, and Janna and David Smith. To my good friend, Michael Rothschild, who read and critiqued every chapter, I am more thankful than he can ever know.

I am especially grateful to two of my old friends, Nancy Adler Baumel and Barbara Marks, who helped me with every single phase of the research: searching through archives at the Rockville Centre Public Library and other archival repositories for historical data and pertinent photographs, reading old newspapers, making contacts, conducting interviews with local sources, checking facts, reading and editing draft pages. This memoir owes a great deal to their cheerful and tireless efforts. Nancy's son, Richard Baumel, was also of great help in researching the 1951 and 1955 Dodger seasons.

To my sisters, Charlotte and Jeanne, who provided countless hours of interviews and a lifetime of love and support, I dedicate this book.

Finally, my deepest thanks to my husband, Richard Goodwin, my best friend and companion, who worked with me at every stage of this work, as he has done with all my previous works, listening to my stories, suggesting themes, editing my words, critiquing my drafts. As a child, I had dreamed of sharing a marriage like that of Carl and Edna Probst, the husband and wife team who ran the corner delicatessen, working side by side all day with no separation of the work place and the living place. With my husband who, like me, writes at home, I have found just such a marriage, except, of course, that we deal in words rather than cold cuts and potato salad.

If you have enjoyed reading this large print book and you would like more information on how to order a Compass Press Large Print Book, please write to:

Wheeler Publishing, Inc.
P.O. Box 531
Accord, MA 02018-0531